WITH THE COMPLIMENTS
OF
MR. NIALL D. HODGE
To
W. S. ALLISON
18 CRAIGBO TERR,
65 BATH STREET, BUCKIE.
GLASGOW, C. 2.

041-332 2488

THE POWER I PLEDGE

WILLIAM QUARRIER

The Power I Pledge

Being a Centenary Study of the
Life of William Quarrier
and
The Work He Pioneered

JAMES ROSS

'He gave me the utmost of my asking, and I felt that I
would need to give Him the utmost of the power I
pledged.'

William Quarrier, 1897

Privately printed for
QUARRIER'S HOMES
by Robert MacLehose & Company Limited
The University Press, Glasgow

Contents

DEDICATED

To All Who Love and Care for Children

Author's Preface

I am glad to have had the opportunity of writing this book. The study of a man of such faith as William Quarrier has done my soul good and I trust the reader will find a like blessing.

Many friends, young and old, have aided me and I thank them.

JAMES ROSS

Glasgow
January–July 1970

CHAPTER 1

Where am I?

THE name is 'Homelea'.

It is a large house, set alongside the entrance to what appears to be a model village. The Avenues are wide and bear curious names, Faith, Hope and Love! To the north, east and west, other large villas are strikingly set in spacious lawns and flower gardens. The Gryffe water flows through the place and from its bridges and banks a boy, even a girl, may fish. Rich pastureland abounds on all sides and when one looks to the south the Kilbarchan Hills dominate the scene. We are some seventeen miles west of Glasgow, several miles between the townships of Kilmacolm and Bridge of Weir.

The houses on which we gaze are built on what were the lands of Nittingshill Farm, the forty acres of which were bought by a Glasgow shoemaker on 26th April 1876, for £89 an acre. At the centre of this community a massive clock tower draws the eye to a fine Church built in the Gothic style. Nearby there is a School and, beyond the school, one sees extensive playing fields. Not immediately visible from where we stand are tradesmen's and gardeners' sheds and outhouses, a Post Office, a shop, a hairdresser's salon, a shoemaker's 'den', a Fire Station, a large garage, a splendid hospital, a modern swimming pool, an immense and up-to-date Recreation Centre, a teenagers' café, a telephone exchange, a doctor's surgery, a minister's vestry, a library, a community centre, a psychologist's consulting room, a laundry, and much else. Apparently associated with this place one can see, in the distance, a group of buildings which turn out to be

Scotland's only Colony of Mercy for those with epilepsy, whilst further to the south-west lies a farm, Hattrick, which belongs here too.

What is this place? What is 'Homelea'?

It is the administrative centre of Quarrier's Homes. For long known as the Orphan Homes of Scotland this Community now bears the name of its Founder, William Quarrier, whose centenary in the work of child care is celebrated during 1971. This house, once Quarrier's own home, is the nerve centre of a vast enterprise, the story of which, in its origins and growth is a continuing miracle. This is a community of children who stand in need and of men and women who are pledged to help them. Over five hundred young people are in residence here, each one with a story to tell of some form of deprivation, many of them unable to count on one person outside this village who cares, but every single one of them aware that here he does count as an individual, and that here he will be supported in times both good and bad. Each child knows that to this place he may turn at any moment in his life for succour or companionship, for encouragement or for guidance, just as instinctively as any person, anywhere, in joy and in sorrow, will turn his face homeward.

In 1864 William Quarrier began work for destitute and orphan children in the City of Glasgow and on 17th September 1878 the ambition of his life came nearer fulfilment in the opening of his national 'Orphan Homes of Scotland' at Bridge of Weir. Since then thousands of boys and girls have lived in its cottages and have been trained in its Church and School. Already in his lifetime (he died in 1903) Mr. Quarrier saw 64 buildings erected at Bridge of Weir, and these included the first Tuberculosis Sanatoria in Scotland. In the City of Glasgow he had premises at Cessnock, and had built, in 1872, a massive Night Shelter and Evangelistic Centre at James Morrison Street. These replaced buildings he had previously rented. Stretching overseas, he had established a centre in Canada to which orphan

children from Scotland went, and from which they were
found homes with families throughout the Dominion.

Ever in advance of his times, William Quarrier planned a
Colony of Mercy for those suffering from Epilepsy and
bought ground for this before his death in 1903. It is still
the only Colony of its kind in the northern Kingdom

To do all this required an enormous amount of money. It
was a big business enterprise, entered on out of compassion
for children and the needy. Quarrier himself was a shoemaker
and not a rich man. He had had no formal education. His
knowledge of the world was limited. In all things, but one, he
was self-taught. The one thing other was something given. It
was Christian Faith. In all the years he laboured he believed
himself to be but an instrument in God's hands. The work
was the Lord's and William Quarrier only His agent. God
would provide. Accordingly there never was an appeal for
money, no bazaars to raise funds, no envelope collections,
no flag day. It was an enterprise of faith from the beginning,
and so it has continued. Never once has its support been in
doubt. Never once has God's provision been withheld.
More than one person, growing somewhat sophisticated in
faith, has come to this place only to be brought back to the
centre of belief, to the things that stand, to the One who is
both able and faithful.

In 1872 William Quarrier issued the first of thirty-one
annual reports on his work, written in his own hand. Entitled
'A Narrative of Facts Relative to Work Done for Christ in
Connection with the Orphan and Destitute Children's
Emigration Homes, Glasgow', it shows immediately the
man's mettle, compassion and ability. From this Narrative
the present-day leaders at Quarrier's Homes date the
beginning of the Founder's life-work, hence the 1971
Centenary Year. With justification they could have dated
Quarrier's task as from the publication of his first letter on
the subject of child need and care, dated 30th November 1864
and published in the *GlasgowHerald*. This led to the formation
of a Shoeblack and Industrial Brigade in the City on 28th

December 1864. Had this date been taken as the beginning then it would have been seen that Mr. Quarrier was almost exactly a contemporary of his equally famous companion in England, Dr. Barnardo, the centenary of whose work was fittingly celebrated in 1966.

However, in such matters, the precise date of beginning matters little and the United Kingdom may well be thankful that around the same time in various places men and women were found to take in hand a work too long neglected.

This, then, is 'Homelea' and this is the man for ever associated with it. His story and all that follows is well worth telling. It is worth knowing. It is worth pondering. This Centenary book will aid this process by seeking to answer in each chapter a different question. The questions form the chapter titles. You must know, however, that this is a dangerous book. It tells a story that is quite incredible on purely human terms. One fact becomes clear as the tale unfolds. It is that the Author of the whole high adventure is One other than man. Before we go on we should think much about this. We should also pray.

CHAPTER 2

When and Why?

WILLIAM QUARRIER was born on 16th September 1829 and died on 16th October 1903. Thus, although in almost every sense a distinct Victorian, he nevertheless lived under four British monarchs, George IV (1820–30), William IV (1830–7), Victoria (1837–1901), and Edward VII (1901–10).

When he was born the United Kingdom was emerging from the Industrial Revolution and just beginning to understand, with justifiable fears in some quarters at least, what this had cost and would continue to cost, many of her people. He lived through a time of awakening social conscience and played a worthy part in its quickening. When he died he had seen the birth and establishment of a new Britain, a land in which the ancient question 'Am I my brother's keeper?' had begun to be answered correctly, 'No, I am my brother's brother.'

Fourteen years before Quarrier's birth the Battle of Waterloo had given Britain hard-won victory, after some sixty-seven years of war out of the hundred and twenty-six years between 1689 and 1815. In a series of seven great European and world wars we had emerged with complete control of the seas and this, in turn, ensured our mastery of India, North America and Australia, not to mention numerous islands which flew the Union Jack. When William Quarrier was a lad of eleven years British rule was acknowledged by more than a tenth of the world's twelve hundred million inhabitants. Yet, at that time, the population of England and Wales was scarcely fifteen million, Ireland eight million and Scotland two and a half millions. The twenty-five and a half million had some responsibility!

The great political names of Quarrier's lifetime bring to mind issues and movements of a bygone age. The Duke of Wellington, Disraeli, Gladstone, Peel, Russell, Palmerston, Stanley, Walpole, Salisbury, Campbell-Bannerman, Joseph Chamberlain, Lord Randolph Churchill, Asquith, Lloyd George, are some of those who served the nation at Westminster during this period. Even the world famous British war leader, Winston Churchill, entered Parliament two years before Quarrier died.

Led by its politicians the country managed to hold on to a time of peace after Waterloo until the Crimean War (1853–5). The Indian Mutiny of 1857 and the American Civil War (1861–65) would disturb the Glasgow of Quarrier's young manhood and the Boer War of 1899–1901 saw a number of his own lads on active service. On 1st June 1902 his Narrative for the year contains this entry :

> This Sabbath Day over the whole Empire thanksgiving is ascending to God that the war in South Africa is over. We pray that the peace proclaimed yesterday may be a lasting one, and that wisdom may be given to the Government to deal with the problems that must be solved and settled ere the pacification of the new colonies can be assured.

It is entirely in keeping with the man that the very next entry in his Narrative begins with the words :

> *2nd June 1902* Amid the rejoicings over the news from South Africa our needs are not forgotten, and from various sources there have reached us £145 15. 8. for the Homes and £4 for the Sanatoria.

The South African War also made its demands on the Homes, as an entry for 17th October 1902 shows :

> Among today's letters is an application from a Major-General in Edinburgh, on behalf of the four children of another victim of the South African War. The mother, alas, is also a victim to a more deadly enemy than war, and the poor children are in dire need of the help which we are, thank God, able to give them.

'In dire need' those three words, were engraved on Quarrier's heart from early childhood. But, when he was born, and for many years before, not many in this country were prepared to do anything to relieve the need. It is more than passing strange that in a land which had achieved great military renown, founded a world-wide Empire, established itself as the leading industrial nation of the earth and conquered the oceans, men and women could daily pass by destitute children, ragged and uneducated adolescents, and many of their fellow creatures impoverished and devoid of hope, seemingly oblivious of their need and, for the most part, studiously unwilling to help.

There was then a great gulf in the nation. The rich were rich and tended to increase their riches. The poor were well-nigh destitute, working incredibly long hours, in desperate conditions, for a pittance. Beginning their working lives whilst yet children of six and seven years, no hope of wealth or advancement lay before them, only an increasing fear of sickness, unemployment, and the dreaded poorhouse. Very few were ever able to overcome such disadvantages. Whilst there must have been much individual compassion little of it has been recorded. The State and Society believed so much in the independence and liberty of the subject that those who sought to enact restrictive legislation that would procure sufficiency for all were doomed to failure. A nation which had abolished slavery throughout British territories in 1807 permitted the slavery of its own children in factory and mine to continue, with but little check, until 1833. Foreigners tend to find the British outlook odd in some respects. Perhaps they are justified when we remember that in Britain, a Society for the Prevention of Cruelty to Animals existed some sixty years before a Society for the Prevention of Cruelty to Children!

One can hardly account for this lack of concern by unawareness of the problem, since poverty and destitution were evident in every town and city, and cried out for attention in every factory and mine. In some measure the acceptance of destitution had become a philosophy.

In 1798 Thomas Robert Malthus, a clergyman, published

B

his 'Essay on the Principle of Population' in which he argued that the population constantly outran the food available and that the economy of the world required nature's law of removing surplus mouths by starvation. This teaching undoubtedly suited many factory-owners and landed proprietors who, to enable their own advancement in wealth, accepted the degradation and hunger of children and workers as an ordering of divine providence. Malthus wrote :

> We are bound in justice and honour formally to disclaim the *right* of the poor to support. To this end I should propose a regulation to be made declaring that no child born from any marriage taking place after the expiration of a year from the date of the law should ever be entitled to parish assistance. . . . A man who is born into a world already possessed, if he cannot get subsistence from his parents on whom he has a just demand, and if the society does not want his labour, has no claim or right to the smallest portion of food and in fact has no business to be where he is. At nature's mighty feast there is no vacant cover for him.

It is proper to say that the Revd. T. R. Malthus was himself a kindly man and that in a later publication he greatly modified his argument. Nevertheless the proposition was not without its effect.

One may question whether many folk in the Glasgow of Quarrier's day would have heard of Malthus, nor perhaps would they have worked out their attitude to destitution in any intellectual way. Yet the need in the city was very great and was largely ignored.

From a population of nearly 13,000 in 1708 Glasgow had increased to some 202,000 inhabitants in the year of Quarrier's birth. By the end of the century the figure had grown to over a million, and Glasgow had become the second city of the Empire. This rapid and continuing growth presented many social problems in the realms of housing, health, employment, care, and social need. The incomers were largely from rural parishes, many arriving from Ireland and the Scottish Highlands. Their former way of life had been quite other than that of a great city and they had left

behind them the sense of belonging, and the natural neigh-
bourliness, of small places. Many could not cope; tuberculosis
and other diseases were rampant, work was often scarce,
drink was cheap, evil and sordidness were not lacking, and
few were about to guide and help. Unwanted children, some
deformed, some illegitimate, practically all hungry, were to
be found in the streets making their poor living in any way
possible. No one was nominated by the State to look after
them, parents being held entirely responsible for their
offspring until 1891, when the 'Custody of Children' Bill
became law, and gave certain rights to any Benevolent
Society, whose bona fides could not be questioned, in regard
to children in their care. In such a situation it was small
wonder that many of those children became delinquents.
Got at by evil men and women in their young days and
taught to steal, lie, and worse, life did not give them much
chance to make good. And always there seemed to be no
one who cared!

But, in the providence of God, relief was on the way, and a
new world for the unwanted child was about to open up. In
all the great cities the situation was desperate. But God had
heard the cry of the children and was to help them right
early.

Already in 1835 a Prussian Pastor, George Müller, aged
thirty, had set up an Orphanage for destitute children in
Bristol. He had worked in that city for several years, had
visited Halle in Germany in January 1835 and had seen the
great Orphanage established there by August Hermann
Francke. At tea in a friend's house on 20th November 1835
he picks up the biography of Francke. This has meaning for
him as, since his visit to Francke's Orphanage, he has often
thought of working in a similar way in Bristol. So he arranges
a public meeting to share his plans. The whole project is to be
a venture of faith and Müller himself makes it clear that
although he yields to no one in compassion for needy children,
his primary purpose is to demonstrate that God does answer
prayer. Prayer is made for the money and equipment

required, for helpers, for premises . . . , and all are forthcoming. The work begins – and continues today.

In London a medical student preparing for missionary
service in China, twenty-one years of age, is teaching in a
Ragged School, love for children shining in his eyes. En-
listing the aid of a few other students he rents a dilapidated
old donkey-shed for half-a-crown a week, cleans it up, puts
in a floor, white-washes the inside, buys and hangs two
paraffin lamps, lights them and gathers within, two nights a
week and on Sundays, 'a crowd of idle, ill-washed, children'
and in this place Dr. Thomas John Barnardo has 'his first
indication of and inspiration towards what proved to be
(his) life's-work'. This happened in July 1867. Just over a
year later a young lad, Jim Jarvis, pleads not to be put out
into the cold at the end of a class meeting. He has no place
to go. Barnardo befriends him, asks if many other children
are homeless, and is told that there are hundreds like Jim.
The Doctor and the destitute lad go together to see where
the others are to be found. On roof-tops, under tarpaulins,
in all sorts of unlikely places homeless boys are trying to
sleep. The sight on one roof-top is best given in Barnardo's
own words :

> There, on the open roof, lay a confused group of boys all asleep.
> I counted eleven. They lay with their heads upon the higher
> part and their feet in the gutter, in as great variety of postures
> as one may have seen in dogs before a fire – some coiled up,
> some huddled two or three together, others more apart. The
> rags that most of them wore were mere apologies for clothes.
> One big fellow appeared to be about eighteen, but the ages of
> the remainder varied, I should say from nine to fourteen.
>
> Just then a cloud passed from the face of the moon, and as
> the pale light fell upon the upturned faces of those sleeping
> boys, and I realised the terrible fact that they were absolutely
> homeless and destitute, and were almost certainly but samples
> of many others, it seemed as though the hand of God himself
> had suddenly pulled aside the curtain which concealed from my
> view the untold miseries of forlorn child-life upon the streets of
> London.

So begins the great enterprise of Barnardo's Homes which is an epic of child care and Christian concern. Like George Müller Dr. Barnardo goes forward in Christian faith. The two men are not alike in other respects and their methods of work differ. Both offered to God their unique gifts which He accepted and used.

Also in London others are at work. Charles Dickens, with a ready pen and a bruised heart, paints the scene in undying words. Lord Shaftesbury's massive achievements are well known. Not so well known, perhaps, but of great value, was the imaginative service of Miss Annie Macpherson who found orphan and destitute children and arranged homes and friends for them in Canada.

Across the country, at Liverpool, Josephine Butler is busy and has, as fellow citizen and partner in all good work for underprivileged youth, the Roman Catholic priest, Father James Nugent.

In Scotland, already in 1815, an Orphanage, which still continues, had been established at Carolina Port, on the banks of the Tay at Dundee. In Aberdeen, in November 1870, the 'Aberdeen Association for Improving the Condition of the Poor' was established and the very next year began child care. In Glasgow Dr. Thomas Chalmers, working from his Kirk at the Tron, had turned many eyes and hands towards the needy poor, and across the country in Edinburgh Dr. Guthrie, another minister, had set up his Ragged Schools.

And through the streets of Glasgow to which he had been brought, a fatherless and impoverished child, from his native Greenock at the age of five years, there walked, haltingly at first, playfully later, and then with manly tread, William Quarrier, the man who, under God, was already chosen for the largest and finest bit of down-to-earth work in the service of unloved children that Scotland has ever known.

Before we look at the man himself and, later, at the work he did, we shall ask another question. Why did all this concern show itself at this particular period ? Was it chance ?

Was it inevitable? Was it part of our social evolution? Was it all this and something more? Was it God?

Looking back we may well feel that, to a large extent, the beginning of such child service was inevitable. Society may close its eyes to its ills for long enough but the time eventually comes when reasonable men and women cannot, and dare not, let the sore fester. To some extent private and national self-interest would dictate policy, and the Victorian conscience was calculated to engender aid sooner or later.

There is no doubt also, that this was part of our country's social evolution. The Industrial Revolution had changed not only the dwellings of men. Their attitudes had also been affected. This was the period when railways came to Britain and, in the cities, electric tramways. In 1839 we get the first bicycle and in 1882 steam trawlers made their appearance. Already in 1895 work had started on a Hydro-Electric scheme at Foyers. The motor car appeared before Quarrier's death and very soon thereafter man took to the air. Easier means of transport meant greater opportunities of travel, more numerous occasions for people to get together and, therefore, a quickening in the give and take of ideas. When men and women did get together there was more than discussion. Complaints were aired, fears were shared, hopes were given words and always, amongst the poor, the one great hope would be that the world would give their children a better deal than it had meted out to the parents. Although poverty restricted the full use of such benefits, nevertheless, social intercourse inevitably speeded up and more people began to dream of a brighter tomorrow.

Yet there was more to it than that. It is remarkable that in different places at around the same period men and women were to be found taking the lead in what was a long-neglected field. When one considers the story of our race the same pattern emerges. A work requires to be done. For long enough the nation ignores the demand although here and there a hardy pioneer makes his voice heard. Then, almost imperceptibly at first, but with gathering momentum and increasing leadership, interest is generated, needs are made known, the task is put in hand and the work develops. Such movements are doubtless inevitable, most are part of our social evolution, yet there remains a mystery. The whole effort can hardly be built on chance. Barnardo, Müller, and Quarrier all unite in saying that in such movements the hand of God is in action. He it is who chooses time and place. He it is who raises up and sends men to the task. They would claim that this is how the Holy Spirit works. In face of the stupendous success attending their labours who can say they are wrong? Certainly in complete and absolute reliance upon God Quarrier planned and executed his work. To this day Christian trust is the acknowledged foundation of life in the village he created. With a refreshing absence of demythologising Quarrier handed the whole adventure over to God in child-like faith. The children were His, were they not? He had sent William Quarrier to their aid. Therefore He would provide. He did. He still does.

In the next chapter we learn more of this man whose life spanned four reigns, whose time was set in a period of great wealth and great destitution, whose compassion for children born out of his own early sufferings, whose business acumen and restless brain fitted him to be Heaven's instrument in Scotland, for the succour of little children in need. It must be added that without the direct and simple trust he had in Jesus Christ, and His promises, no chapter of this book could have been written.

CHAPTER 3

Who was William Quarrier?

ALONGSIDE many Scottish highways during the winter a sign may be seen, 'Grit for the road.' The broken stone and rubble help to keep a vehicle on the move in difficult places and allow many a stranded car to make a new beginning. Men need another kind of grit for the roadway of life, since life also has its stormy passages and occasional full stops. This grit, or inner courage, appears sometimes to be given. In other lives it is acquired. Alas! In some cases it is conspicuously absent.

William Quarrier had this quality built into his nature. When about 8 years of age and a shoemaker's apprentice at Paisley he was keen to spend Hogmanay and New Year at home in Glasgow with his mother and sisters. There was no money for the coach so, in his bare feet, he took to the road and faced up to its seven miles. On the outskirts of the town the stage-coach caught up with the young hiker. Perhaps as a bit of mischief, perhaps as a bit of show-off, perhaps simply because he wanted to keep warm, the young lad began to run alongside. He persisted in this. The passengers took notice and, in admiration, threw some pennies to the runner. When they reached the Half-Way House William, richer by 11½d., was invited to eat with them. For the next half of the journey the passengers insisted on the apprentice joining them in the coach, and paid his fare. Thus early was determination shown with, perhaps, just a tiny promise of the sagacity which was to mark his life. Certainly the right kind of grit was not lacking.

His story until then was a normal one for the early 19th century. His father, another William Quarrier, worked as a ship's carpenter sometimes at home in Greenock and now and again on board ship travelling to foreign ports. Greenock, when Quarrier was born, was a thriving and growing town. It had already given men of renown to the world including James Watt of steam-engine fame and John Galt the author. No one could have foreseen on 16th September 1829 that the baby born in Cross Shore Street to the ship's carpenter and Annie Booklass, his wife, would become a household name of honour in Scotland, and beyond, in days to come. Wealth and poverty are relative terms. A man whose father never earned more than some £7 a week is amazingly rich, in his own eyes at least, when he can count on a regular £20 a week of income. Likewise in another sphere, a leader in industry or commerce may feel himself impoverished when he becomes a Cabinet Minister and has to make do on the appropriate salary! In his own day William Quarrier senr. was, doubtless, comfortable as a ship's carpenter and would be able to maintain his wife and three children decently. Young William was the middle child and the only son. Death robbed the family of the bread-winner and plunged them into all the hardships of Victorian poverty. The carpenter fell victim to the scourge of cholera and in 1832 died at Quebec during one of his voyages. It is difficult for us today to understand just what this would mean to the widow and her children. The day of the Welfare State was not yet. There was no widow's pension and no family allowance. There was Poor Relief, but mighty little of that, and as a last resort the Poorhouse itself. From the latter the poorest of the poor shrank with loathing. To enter such a place was the unspeakable last word in terms of human dignity and endeavour, and all means were taken to avoid this termination of hope. Like most mothers in such a position Mrs. Quarrier had to fend for herself and her children with her own hands and brain. A small shop was opened in Greenock but there was no success. What could be done? The nearby city of Glasgow had more opportunity and to it she set off in search of work and a new life. William Quarrier was then five

years of age and one of his earliest memories was of the
struggle to get enough money together to pay the steamboat
fares.

Glasgow was no Utopia either. The first home was in
Main Street, Gorbals. From there they went to a house in a
High Street close. The area had already degenerated into
slum property and conditions were far from pleasant. Often
there must have been a tear in the mother's eye and, certainly,
the children were frequently hungry. There was much evil
around, life was both hard and grim, drink was cheap and
offered a quick means of release from the terrors of sobriety.
Children were hardly protected and to this extent, even
under the façade of 19th-century social respectability, 'per-
missiveness' already reigned. Quarrier himself was to say
later that as he looked back he realised it was only the
good hand of the Lord upon him in childhood which saved
him from evil. He saw many of his contemporaries ruined in
health and prospect and confessed, 'That I was not also led
in the same way I owe to God's overruling and preserving
care.' Perhaps his own grit had something to do with it.

Mrs. Quarrier found work, taking in fine sewing. Her son
acted as message boy and was much on the move. He even
did some of the sewing when there was a rush at home. But
the pittance his mother was able to earn in this way was never
adequate to her needs and often the children were miserable.
Something of this comes out in William Quarrier's own
words. In the first 'Narrative of Facts' concerning his work
for children, issued in 1872, he looks back on his own
beginnings :

> When a little boy, I stood in the High Street of Glasgow, bare-
> footed, bareheaded, cold and hungry, having tasted no food for a
> day and a half, and, as I gazed at each passer-by, wondering
> why they did not help such as I, a thought passed through my
> mind that I would not do as they when I would get the means
> to help others.

Mrs. Quarrier was not then a religious woman and the lad
had, at that time, only a smattering of Christian knowledge,

such as would come from the occasional visit to a mission Sunday School. Yet here is displayed real compassion and a sense of dedication. Born of bitter experience the vow is made and never forgotten. The workman is already being trained for his life of special service. The will is being tensed and the heart made warm. But for William Quarrier such understanding is afar off. Indeed when, at mission Sunday School, he hears and sings of the 'happy land, far, far away' and the loving Heavenly Father who cares for all, he takes leave to wonder why such a good Father does not send someone at that very moment to make Scotland a happier land. Here are his own words :

I wished that the land was here and the happiness now!

The memory of that day with its hunger, its misery, its questionings and its vow, never left Quarrier. Just as in the worst part of the battlefield a soldier may have an experience which alters the path of his whole life and remains a point of constant reference thereafter so, in this extreme of dejection, in this most miserable of surroundings, God speaks to the young lad and, although William knew it not, light and purpose were already being shed on his way. Later he is to liken himself to Moses going down to lead his children from the land of bondage. Here, then, is Moses awakening to their needs, Moses becoming their champion, although a long wilderness experience of preparation still lies ahead.

In the course of the years another vital experience shapes the man. At the age of seventeen Quarrier is converted, quietly, to Christian faith. His dearest wish is to see his mother likewise committed. His first efforts are unavailing but over a period of years he prays for this to take place. Doggedly he does battle with his Lord and at the end his prayer is answered, his mother accepts Christ. Out of this deep and persistent prayer, and its result, a strong and calm faith in God and in the power of intercession is born. From this moment onwards he is never in any doubt that if the work to which he sets his hand at any time is according to

God's will it must succeed. He takes then as his motto 'Have Faith in God'. Today, a flower bed, alongside the great children's church at the Homes he set up, annually witnesses to this truth and the words of the text, written in flowers, are there for all to read and ponder.

The whole foundation of all Quarrier's work lies in these two experiences. In them he discovered a spiritual rock from which nothing was ever able to move him. Compassion, dedication and complete trust are to mark all he does to the very end of his days.

But at the point we have reached William is still the poor young lad of Glasgow's High Street. Before he is seven he is at work fixing large heads to the fashionable pins of the age. He works twelve hours a day and brings home one shilling a week! Today, for that sum, one can scarcely buy a loaf of bread. Then, it was a lad's weekly wage. Even such a small sum was of help to his struggling mother. Soon he leaves this job to begin his apprenticeship. So far as can be learned he never attends any school. At seven years of age he is an apprentice shoemaker in Glasgow. The firm he begins with fails, so he moves on to Paisley. There he does well and at the astonishingly early age of twelve years he is a journeyman.

For a few years thereafter Quarrier moves around several Glasgow shops, perfecting his trade and gathering experience. It says much for his mother's wisdom and his own steadfastness of character that already he carries the hallmark of a tradesman.

When he was nearly seventeen he went to the Argyle Street shop of Mrs. Hunter to seek work. Mrs. Hunter was a keen Glasgow business woman. She was also a devout Baptist who had a great concern for those who worked for her, especially if they showed signs of good character and steadiness. These she soon discovered in the young shoemaker she now employed. His diligence, punctuality, and good craftmanship spoke volumes and soon she was thinking of his religious wellbeing. In time she asked if he attended any church and was told that he did not do so. She asked him to go with her to Blackfriars Street Baptist Church where she was a member. William went with her and it was there he was converted. He tells of it thus :

> When about seventeen years of age my mother and I were invited by a devoted Christian lady to go to church, and I there (listen to this – seventeen years of age), I there, for the first time, heard the great truth of the Gospel, that 'God so loved the world that He gave His only begotten Son, that whosoever believeth on Him should not perish but have everlasting life.' Under the influence of the Spirit of God, and the teaching of the Word of God, I was led to accept of Christ as all my salvation.

There it stands, prosaic almost, in words. No crisis is recorded, no noise and tumult, no written conviction of sin, no flights of rhetoric or fancy. The bald truth, the solemn acceptance, the total commitment, these are given, and the life he had always tried to live well, is now in conscious harness with the power of God as shown in Jesus of Nazareth.

He was admitted to church membership on 25th February 1852, served for a while as beadle and was active in bringing others to his Saviour. In 1863 he left Blackfriars Church and became associated with Hope Street (now Adelaide Place) Baptist Church. He was elected a deacon there in 1868 and for the rest of his life he was part of the life and work of this congregation, sharing its worship, assisting its ministers, and playing a full part in its many evangelistic activities.

Soon after his conversion William found his thoughts turning towards the Christian ministry but by and by he was convinced that his particular task did not lie in that field. So, alongside his Christian service, he continued to excel in his own trade and to praise the Lord in the goodness of the boots he made. From time to time thoughts of the impoverished children of the streets came to him and he did not forget his early vow. The means to begin work for the needy little ones was not immediately to hand so he planned his own business career, ever with the determination that one day he would be their friend and helper. When he was 23 years of age he set up in business on his own.

In the meantime another power had entered his life. He had fallen in love with his employer's daughter, Isabella Hunter. A great love has been known to shape a man's sense of mission in life and Quarrier was blessed in that Isabella shared to the full his Christian concern and his particular devotion to unwanted and deprived children. Had it been otherwise all the great work he did would have been hindered, if not left undone.

On 2nd December 1856 William and Isabella were married at 5 Douglas Street, Glasgow, by the Revd. Dr. James Paterson of Hope Street Baptist Church. William was 27 years of age. By this time he had seen his business grow to such an extent that two moves to more extensive premises had been required. From Piccadilly Street in Anderston he had gone to Argyle Street and then to Madeira Buildings further along the same street. Soon he was to develop his work and he became one of the first multiple-shop owners in Glasgow, eventually having business premises in three different places.

By 1864 the name of William Quarrier was well known in a number of Glasgow circles. He had made a place for himself in the business community. In church life he had shown ability and initiative. In addition to the support he gave his own congregation he was one of the founders of Dunoon and Kilmarnock Baptist Churches, had promoted various evangelistic campaigns in Glasgow and had helped to bring to the city a number of prominent 19th-century preachers. He showed some interest in political issues and was to be found on the side of William Ewart Gladstone. His business associates and church friends looked upon him as an able and eager citizen who, with his wife and children, set an example of Christian living both within their hospitable home and outside in the larger community. It would appear to the onlooker that the thirty-five-year-old business man was set fair towards an increasing prosperity and an increasing influence in commercial, church and civic affairs. No one could have guessed that within eighteen years all Quarrier's material possessions would be hazarded in a great act of heart-warming faith.

November is not one of Scotland's best months for weather. One cold wintry evening William Quarrier is making his way home from business along Jamaica Street. In front of him stands a young match-seller of the streets, the tears welling in his eyes. Quarrier's compassion is aroused. He stops, asks the boy why he cries, and is told that someone has stolen the lad's entire stock of matches and his money. The man gives the boy enough to replenish his tray and goes on his way. Who can tell what thoughts are in Quarrier's mind? Some thirty years ago he had stood at the kerb too, hungry and miserable. The vow taken then and not forgotten presses on his soul with an urgency that cannot be gainsaid. But what can be done for such children? In what way can they be helped? What can he do himself? Where is the money to be found for such work as would be involved in complete child-care? Do the children themselves want the kind of life that Quarrier covets for them? Would the citizens of Glasgow understand his aims? What would be the attitude of the authorities? Does not this work require to be done on a national scale and, if so, ought it not to stem from Government sources? What of his wife, children, and the three orphan children of his deceased younger sister and her husband, whom they are now bringing up? And yet, the need is great and Quarrier has no doubt that God has laid this work on his soul. What is to be done? Quarrier takes up his pen and writes to the Editor of the *Glasgow Herald* the following letter, which is published on 2nd December:

Glasgow,
30th November, 1864.
Sir,
    On my occasional visits to London I have been much pleased with many of the sights to be seen there, but with none more than with the tidy and clean appearance of the London Shoe-

Black Brigade, an institution peculiar to London. There are to be seen many hundreds of youths who have none to care for them, fed, clothed and educated from their own earnings, in brushing boots and shoes, and sent forth to the world to be useful members of society. No doubt many of these youths, if left to themselves, would become wrecks on the great sea of London life, but as it is they are an honour to the nation for industry and perseverance, and these good results may be chiefly attributed to those gentlemen who give a little of their spare time to the management of the Society.

Always on my return to Glasgow I have wished that we had such an institution here. I think we have need of it. In almost every street of our city are to be found youths who have none to care for them and possessing all the elements of industry and perseverance. If these were formed into a Glasgow Shoe-Black Brigade the same results as have followed the London institution might be fairly looked for here.

Now, sir, if a number of gentlemen would come forward (which I am sure many would be glad to do), I would be happy to be one of them, giving of my time and substance towards this object. I have no doubt, with the aid of your pen and that of your contemporaries, of the success of such an undertaking. Although it might not have an annual revenue of £40,000 like the Great Western Cooking Depot Scheme, yet, if it fed, clothed and educated forty destitute youths, preserving them from the vices that surround them, and making them useful members of society, I say that the result would far transcend any pecuniary aid that might be given to it.

Quarrier signed the letter 'Shoeblack' but in a P.S. wrote :

I enclose my card with address which you are at liberty to show to any gentleman who may wish to co-operate with me in the above scheme.

Other letters followed to and from William Quarrier. Meetings took place, people became interested, imagination was stirred and, eventually, a Shoe-Black Brigade was formed. From now onwards Mr. Quarrier's life and work merge. The story of the one is the story of the other and in the great days ahead the man and the movement are inseparable.

S.S. *James Arthur*, Quarrier's Homes

CHAPTER 4

What did he do for Glasgow's Children?

Just as the great Nile, before reaching the sea, is divided into the waters of its Delta, only to be united once more in and with the greater Mediterranean, so the life of William Quarrier now moves forward.

His constant flow of interest is the care of young folk but, in the fourteen years between 1864 when he wrote to the *Glasgow Herald* and 1878, when he opened his first cottage homes for orphans at Nittingshill, Bridge of Weir, his activities are so varied, his centres of work so diverse, and his fertile brain and spirit so searching, that this may well be described as his 'Delta time'.

The strength of his concern now channels out ways of service which, indeed, changed the Glasgow scene. A Shoe-black Brigade, a News Brigade, a Parcels Brigade, all speedily formed in business-like fashion, fuse into a Quarrier-controlled unit to become known as The Industrial Brigade.

The rescue of young and old from material want and spiritual ignorance, along with Christian outreach in neighbourhood mission, next claimed his attention and led to the building of large mission premises in James Morrison Street.

Always, the plight of the orphan and destitute child dominated his mind and at the end of those fourteen years, he has the thrill of seeing his first Cottage Homes opened in the lush farmland between Bridge of Weir and Kilmacolm, Renfrewshire.

Henceforth, although they continue for some time to be visible, the Delta streams are united in the waters of deep

c

love and simple faith which carry forward the Orphan
Homes project. A more unified and an even more powerful
William Quarrier appears.

It is difficult for the mind to grasp clearly the variety and
ramifications of the vast enterprise on which the young
shoemaker now embarks. In addition to all the work already
on his shoulders his day must now include committee
meetings, the renting, purchasing and building of property,
negotiations with private individuals and organisations,
contacts with Glasgow Town Council, and the initiation and
carrying through of evangelical missions.

Soon one-third of his own business is given up. A second
third is disposed of in 1879, and in 1882 he quits business
altogether and lives, as his orphan children do, in complete
trust in God.

Through it all his annual Narratives show a single-
minded concern for each individual, each deprived and needy
child. Far ahead of his time, the Diaries of Admission to his
Homes give a day-by-day detailed account of each child. The
attention is painstaking and very human. The background of
each, so far as can be found out, is entered, family relation-
ships are noted and, where possible, interested parties are
visited. The child's own story is always checked. There is a
medical report on each, the educational standard is given and,
often, vivid and humorous notes on the little one's attitudes,
characteristics and behaviour are put down. He knew no
Department of Social Studies, had no Child Care tuition,
but it is doubtful if even the most up-to-date of our modern
Colleges could teach the compassionate shoemaker very
much! What is quite evident is that he saw each child as
being of great worth in himself *at that particular time* and
not simply as an embryo adult, although the future was never
lost sight of either. The child who came under his care was
unique, bearing the marks of Heaven as well as, only too
often, the scars of earth. He was God's child in need of help
and God had sent Quarrier to help. It was as simple and
wonderful as that.

The very diversity of work we now look at makes it difficult to hold the full picture in one's mind and, although they overlap and inter-penetrate each other in terms of time, place, and importance, we shall consider what was accomplished under two sections in this chapter :

(a) the Industrial Brigades of Glasgow, and
(b) the Refuge and Mission Outreach in the same city.

The establishing of the National Orphan Homes (now Quarrier's Homes) in the city, later at Cessnock, and then at Bridge of Weir; the vision and labour required to fit out and send six thousand, six hundred and eighty-seven children to Canada; and the setting up of the first Tuberculosis Sanatoria in Scotland and the first and, so far, only Colony for those suffering from epilepsy in the country, will give matter enough for the next chapter.

(a) The Industrial Brigade

As a result of the letter in the *Glasgow Herald* of 30th November 1864 a Committee of responsible men was set up and soon £100 was gathered to enable a Shoeblack Brigade to begin. Quarrier soon found that although he had good support he would have to shoulder most of the work himself.

Shoeblack boys were already to be seen at work in the city's railway stations and in the streets but, of course, they were in no way organised and had many problems. Quarrier now sought them out and invited them to tea at his home in Kingston Place. Some forty or fifty lads did come and had, probably, the best tuck-in of their lives. The idea of a Shoeblack Brigade was explained to them. They would wear a uniform of cap, navy-blue jacket trimmed with red, a red badge on the arm, and dark trousers. Each would be provided with a box of brushes, blacking, and all that was required for the job. They would be united in their work and would respect each other. Each lad would keep 8d. out of every 1s. earned and the fourpence would be paid into a common fund from which all the shoeblacks' needs would be met. In addition they would be required to attend a night school to be set up and expected to attend a Sunday School.

The good William had some disappointment that evening. Only some fourteen boys proved willing to join his Brigade and, alas!, when the guests had gone it was discovered that a number of family articles had accompanied them! But he was not unduly cast down and with the first few the Shoeblack Brigade was put into operation. Eventually there was to be a corps of about two hundred shoeblacks a year in the city streets, all wearing the distinctive uniform. Premises were found in Jamaica Street as a first HQ and night school. The rent here proved too much and a move was made to Bath Street. For two years this was the centre until the growth of Shoeblack and allied work made it necessary to find larger accommodation. This was found at 114 Trongate. It consisted of the entire floor of a building and comprised six apartments. Here it was also possible to lodge some twenty or thirty boys who had nowhere else to live. The rent was £40 p.a. and a ten years' lease was taken.

Soon Quarrier was turning his attention to another section of Glasgow's young, unprivileged life. To be seen in the streets after the newspapers came out were many youngsters, grubby, sticky, and uncared for, hawking their copies. Quickly they, too, were organised and a News Brigade came into being. Since those children began their work later in the day a morning school was arranged for them. By and by, in their Jamaica Street premises, presided over by a Superintendent and Matron, some hundred boys of the News Brigade learn the three Rs and are sent out to sell their papers, clean, tidy, and disciplined.

Within a year of the formation of the Shoeblack Brigade the third of the groups came into being. This was the Parcels Brigade. Wearing a canvas tunic, black belt and a special badge, the lads of this Brigade would offer to carry parcels for the citizens at a rate of 2d. for half-a-mile and 3d. a mile. Further, the parcels carried had their safe delivery guaranteed by the Brigade. The parcel was handed over, the lad's number taken and the rest was in order. It says much for the honesty and sense of fair-play shown by the slum laddies of Glasgow that never once during the life of the Parcels Brigade did any claim require to be made.

Soon the premises at 114 Trongate became the GHQ of all three Brigades and became known as The Industrial Brigade Home. It was well established as such by 1868 when the Prince and Princess of Wales (later Edward VII and Queen Alexandra) passed along the Trongate. Arrangements to lower a silver casket containing a loyal address from the lads of the Brigades into the royal carriage went awry, but the casket and Address were duly delivered at Marlborough House, and a kindly letter of acknowledgement cheered the 'Brigadier General' on his way.

All this is, of course, largely adminstrative, but the main concern was the help given the boys themselves. What an uplift came into their lives! A sense of togetherness, common enterprise, pride in body and clothes, an increasing knowledge, and the constant influence of a good Christian life, all this was brought to bear on each boy and many lives were permanently enriched.

For many years the lads of the Industrial Brigades were kenspeckle figures in Glasgow. Inevitably there were difficulties. Vested interests opposed the organisation of the young vendors. The already licensed City Porters were not too happy to have the Parcels Brigade operating in competition. There were problems in connection with newspaper supplies for the members of the News Brigade and so on. One way to overcome this opposition and to surmount the problem was for the Town Council to make provision, and take authority, for all children trading on the streets. This had already been done in Liverpool. Quarrier, and others, urged Glasgow Town Council to do this when putting forward their Omnibus Bill of 1895. But other interests were also at work and the Council voted 29 for and 29 against the move. The provision sought was lost on the casting vote of the Lord Provost. On the evening of this decision that gentleman was due to preside at an annual meeting in connection with Quarrier's work. From a study of Quarrier one would gather that he did not beat about the bush and it is no surprise to read that, having 'accidentally' met the Lord Provost late that afternoon, he speedily excused the first citizen of Glasgow from his evening duties! The founder of the Brigades was incensed not to get the support of the city leaders in work which kept the lads well occupied, advanced them in knowledge, served the citizens, and saved many a young life from destitution and evil. However, the Council's decision did not bring the Brigades to an end. Against continuing difficulties they continued to function for a number of years yet. Then changes in education, in social conditions and in the organisation of labour inevitably led to their dissolution.

When they ceased a notable bit of work in Scotland's largest city came to an end. A gallant vision had been transformed into a notable success.

(b) The Refuge and Mission Outreach in Glasgow

Now let William Quarrier speak for himself.

At the end of September 1872 he published his first 'Narrative of Facts'. His Brigades are eight years old, more or less. His work for orphans has made a tentative beginning which we shall look at in the next chapter but still his searching mind leads him to somewhat different work. This is how he puts it:

> Work done for Christ suggests the need of doing more. There are one or two projects which have been before my mind for some time – *1st.* the establishment of a Widow's Help Society, where work would be given to them, such as they might be able for, and remuneration given for the work done, and by this means foster the desire for self-help, which should be the motive principle of all true charity. . . . When they should be gathered at their work, religious subjects could be brought before them by the friends who would meet with them on these occasions, so that when they are working for the bread that perisheth, the bread of life might be offered to them also; *2nd.* the establish-

ment of a Street Boys' Lodging House or Night Refuge where, for a trifling sum, they would be lodged for the night, and have wholesome and moral influence brought to bear on their wild and chequered life; and *3rd.* the establishment of a mission for abandoned women, thieves, and discharged criminals, where the gospel would be preached to them, and help given where found practicable, according to the means placed at our disposal. For the accomplishment of these objects we have secured premises, the rent of which is provided for. It is a portion of the old church situated at the head of Dove Hill, bordering on Graeme Street. It is in the centre of a locality which has much need of light being shed on its moral darkness. £100 will be needed for alterations, furniture and fittings. A portion of this sum has been already sent in; and we have no doubt that God will dispose the hearts of His people to send in what is wanting for this, as well as carry on the mission work, and also for the helping of the orphan and destitute.

Quarrier set his mind on opening this centre at Dove Hill, free of debt, on Hogmanay 1872. As the last days of the year approached it seemed unlikely that the £100 would be forthcoming. At the end of November the sum in hand totalled £49. By 24th December it had risen to £94 5s. 6d. On the 28th it was still only £95 5s. 6d. In William Quarrier's words :

Doubt said 'call on some of your friends, and put the case before them, and you will get all you need', but God said 'Whatsoever ye desire, in prayer, believing, ye shall receive', and so we took the matter to Him . . . we were sorely tempted to give the £5 to make up the sum, but faith said it would come and, on the evening of the 31st. the £5 was sent from a dear friend with an encouraging letter.

So, in the gallery of this old church £100 provided a Kitchen, a Dormitory and a Hall able to seat 400 folk. From this place a 19th-century 'Tell Glasgow' campaign began and was continued with increasing usefulness. Prominent evangelists were brought to the city and often had to move from Dove Hill to larger halls to tell the glad news. All the folk mentioned in Quarrier's 1872 'Narrative' were cared for, and many others. A band of friends aided William in open-air preaching and house-to-house visitation. A school and a Reading Room were set up. In the first ten months 2,137 homeless children had been given lodging, widows had found work and income, discharged prisoners were given hope and, often, work; and scores of God's little ones and poor ones had been fed, clothed, and led to the One in whose Name all was undertaken.

For two years, alongside his other work, Quarrier laboured here almost without rest. Then the School Board bought the premises and it was necessary to look elsewhere for a Mission Centre. About this time Moody (of Moody and Sankey fame) wrote to the *North British Daily Mail* of his concern for some of Glasgow's most needy children. Quarrier answered in a published letter, telling what was already being done, and elaborating his plans for the future.

If £3,000 were forthcoming, he said, a first-class building could be erected at the heart of the city and hundreds of the class about whom Mr. Moody was concerned would be helped and blessed. Two days after his letter Mr. Quarrier announced that the £3,000 had been given. Negotiations then proceeded and on 3rd February 1876 a fine building was opened, fully furnished, and ready for service. To become known as the City Orphan Home the building covered an area of 500 square yards, with a frontage of 72 feet to James Morrison Street and 60 feet to St. Andrew's Square. It was built to last and to serve – all five storeys of it!

In addition to carrying on all the work previously centred in the Dove Hill building lodging was provided here for a hundred working lads, temporary accommodation for sixty homeless children and forty girls between the ages of fourteen and twenty-five.

This building was to become the HQ of much experimental Christian service. Its large Hall was to be filled regularly with enquiring, as well as worshipping, folk and great numbers of Glasgow Christians came to regard it as the centre of their faith's practical application.

The total cost of the City Orphan Home was £7,500

and this sum was given by two ladies in memory of a loved husband and father. Later they raised their gift to a total of £12,000.

For many years after Quarrier's death the City Orphan Home served Glasgow and its people. By 1937, however, social and religious conditions and needs had changed so much it was recognised that other methods and a different type of service were required. The building was then sold. However, the name of Quarrier was not left without a witness in the City which had profited so much from his labours. With part of the proceeds from the sale of the James Morrison Street building a house, 'Overbridge', was bought at Dumbreck Road and organised as a Home for apprentice lads. It served as such for a number of years and is now one of the Quarrier family cottages.

CHAPTER 5

What did he do for Scotland's Children?

THE 'Letters to the Editor' columns in the press form, over the years, a vast mine of information on the questions that interest men from day to day. They give a clear indication of current attitudes, needs, ambitions, and eccentricities. All fields of life are covered and here, often for the first time, men put into written form the dreams and visions that haunt their souls. William Quarrier made full use of this means.

On 1st September 1871, the *Glasgow Herald* and the *North British Daily Mail* carried the following letter over his signature:

Bedford Place,
Glasgow,
August 29th. 1871.

Sir,

For many years past I have been deeply impressed with the necessity that exists here for a home for destitute boys, and I am persuaded that no one who moves about and notices the habits and surroundings of the boys of our streets but will be convinced that such a home is needful. Many of your readers may not be aware of the vast number of houseless and homeless boys who receive shelter in our Night Asylum, and as this is one reason why we should have a home, I beg to put before them the number who have received shelter during the past year which is given in the report at 3397, giving three nights to each boy (which is the allotted time in that institution). This would give the number of 1137 boys who either roam our streets or country without a home to cheer their desolate lives, or a house to cover their defenceless heads.

Some have an easy way of getting out of their Christian

responsibilities, and they say of these helpless ones : 'Send them to the poorhouse'; others, to quiet their consciences, give a copper when they see the haggard face and tattered garments of the little urchin, and so the stream of neglected children goes on, deepening and deepening until God only knows what length it may reach. Fellow Christians and fellow citizens, should such things continue? I would say no, and thus I plead for a home to which any boy may be sent, his case inquired into, and a helping hand extended to him, until he was fit to labour for himself. It is only by such means that crime can be lessened in our juvenile population, for criminals are of the worst class who are so from their youth, and cost a thousand times more for the cure than for the prevention of crime; in fact, I believe it can't be cured, but I am sure it might be prevented, not to speak of the disgrace to us that so many destitute children should be allowed to roam as they like, without let or hindrance.

The amount of help rendered to the destitute boys of our streets by the Shoe-Black Society has been of great use to them, and many hundreds have received help which has been a blessing to themselves and the community, but our great want has been a home to which orphan and destitute boys might be sent at once by any citizen who found them so, to which an emigration scheme might be attached, so as to draft off to another land, all who are fitted for it. Miss Macpherson of London has promised her practical co-operation and with such help there is no fear of success. I have no faith in large institutions where hundreds are ruled with a stringent uniformity which eats out the individuality of its members; but I have great faith in a home where not more than 100 are placed together, and where the individuals would be cared for and watched over by a motherly and fatherly love. The home I think we should begin with might cost from £1,000 to £2,000 to purchase and fit out, and if any of my fellow-citizens would feel inclined to put out this sum, or any amount towards it, I feel certain that it would be laying up treasure in Heaven, where neither moth nor rust doth corrupt, and the blessing of those who are ready to perish would be sure to fall on their heads. The establishment of such a home at the present time would be a fitting stone of remembrance of the Earl of Shaftesbury's visit to our city, and I have no doubt would meet with his hearty support and co-operation. Any communications or subscriptions towards the above object shall be duly acknowledged by

Yours truly,
W. Quarrier.

The letter, and the plan given in it, was no hasty concoction. From the beginning, as we have seen, Quarrier's mind had been set on some such project and all that had gone before was but a training for this work. He had been spurred on the preceding May when, in the house of friends, he had met Miss Annie Macpherson, of whom we have already heard and who was active in arranging for destitute children to find good homes in Canada. They had talked together of Scotland's deprived children and both had agreed that something must be done for them along the lines Quarrier suggested. It was made clear that his friends expected the already busy shoe-maker to take up this work. But he was uncertain, not of his call to the task, but of the time and means available at that moment. For three months he pondered the question. For him prayer was as real as the air he breathed and it was in prayer that he sought guidance. Finally he felt it right to make a first move, under God, and to await results. He says:

> ... after three months' waiting and considering I came to the conclusion that if God wished me to enter on this work, I would take it as a sign from Him that if He sent me from £1,000 to £2,000 for the building of a house for the commencement of the scheme, I would go forward with it. After committing the subject to God in prayer, I resolved to be guided by the answer He sent. . . .

So the letter of 29th August came to be published.

Several questioning days were to pass before the sign was given, but when it came there was no doubting its validity. A few small sums had come in, and these pointed in the right direction. Then the post brought from London the following communication:

85 Gracechurch Street, EC,
London, 12th. September, 1871.

Dear Sir,

I have to thank you for your kindness in calling my attention to your interesting letter respecting a proposed Home for the little boys of Glasgow.

I feel that the public are greatly indebted to you for the

amount of personal work you are willing to undertake in carrying out so benevolent a movement; and if you indicate a suitable building or site I will be glad to invest from £1,000 to £2,000 in purchasing or building a suitable house, and in placing it at your disposal, free of rent, for a number of years, so as fully to test the practicability of your scheme.

If you can more conveniently secure a lease of a suitable building, it will be quite agreeable to me to undertake to pay for several years any rent not exceeding one hundred pounds (£100) per annum.

I remain, Dear Sir,
Yours faithfully,
Thomas Corbett.

No copy of Mr. Quarrier's letter to Mr. Corbett exists 'calling (his) attention' to this proposal, so it is difficult to say how far Quarrier himself made it possible for the Lord to give the sign which he awaited! Such speculation does not, of course, in any way dim the halo, since the Christian is plainly expected to be as eident about His Father's business as are the men of this world about their affairs. Clearly, however, this was the way Quarrier wanted to go. Equally clearly, the years have shown it was also God's way.

Premises from which to begin this new venture were found at 10 Renfrew Lane. Space was limited and work was, to some extent, hindered. Yet lessons were learned and Renfrew Lane has its place in the tale we unfold. The beginning of the National Orphan Homes' story is best told in Quarrier's moving words. In his first 'Occasional Paper', giving a report on his work, he writes :

The Home was commenced in a large room in Renfrew Lane, intended for a workshop, a kitchen partitioned off and the bare, brick walls brightened with Scripture texts etc. On the 18th. of November 1871, the first boy, jacketless and shoeless, came in. We well remember his suspicious look as he inquired whether any more boys would sleep there that night for, if not, he would rather go back to the Brigade. Enticed by the genial warmth of the fire, stripped of his dripping rags, and comfortably clothed, he soon began to feel more at home. But Andrew had no love for solitude, and, in a day or two, he gladly welcomed his first companion, Willie D., a poor orphan boy in a miserable state of rags and vermin. Looking as he is now, bright and happy, though somewhat hasty still, we can hardly realise that it is the same boy whose fearful outbursts of passion, in those early days of our work, filled us with dismay.

Our third boy was Jimmy G., a little waif in our great city, fatherless and motherless, deserted by uncle and aunt at eight years of age; earning his own living by selling matches, standing on his head for a halfpenny, and by other modes more questionable. We well remember Jim's odd little figure, with his ragged clothes pinned around him, and the trusting smile with which he looked at us, and round on the gas-lit room, with hammocks ranged around the walls. Jim was brought to us at the Home by the Matron of one of the Cooking Depots, the stair of which he had haunted. Indeed, with all his knocking about, the little fellow did not seem to have suffered from want of food.

One day, in the beginning of December, three boys came in together. One of them, James S., had not slept in a bed for months before coming into the Home – lying down at night near some furnace fires at the Blochairn Iron Works. Poor fellow, he was suffering, when taken in, from a very sore ankle, burned by a piece of hot iron. It was a great pleasure to the boys when the first little girl was brought into the Home, Sarah P., a poor frightened-looking child of six, who all day long had been shut up in a room alone since her mother's death three months before. Maggie T. was a little Citizen seller of ten years of age, shaggy and uncouth, but with a yearning to be loved and cared for that made her beg to be taken in weeks before we could do so. There are two little sisters, Helen and Isabella M., whose story is a very touching one. Their father was killed some two years since, when employed building the new College, and, strangely enough, their mother dropped down dead when cleaning one of the rooms of the same building a few weeks ago. The passionate grief of Helen (nine years old) when brought in was very sad to see, and she is still suffering in health from what she then passed through, though much comforted now by the presence of the little four-year old Bella, and by feeling that she is again in a real home. One day she brought tears to the Matron's eyes by telling how the Minister broke to her the news of her mother's death, saying the Good Shepherd had taken her mother home to Himself, but if she loved Him He would take care of her. 'And it has come true', Helen said, 'for He has brought me here.'

One of our boys had, for three weeks after his mother's death, wandered homeless in the streets, sleeping on stairs, till he was found at a Mission meeting, crying with hunger, and brought to the Home. Two others had been 'dawsing' (sleeping out) among the egg boxes at the quay, when they heard of the Home, and begged to be taken in. Two brothers and a sister were brought by a Bible-woman from the High Street, so attenuated with starvation that we could hardly look at them without tears.

Such were the first children in the Orphan Homes of Scotland. This brief recital of their condition, background and needs, suffices to show how necessary was Quarrier's work.

Mr. Thomas Corbett, the man used to give the sign for which Quarrier had waited, was a Scots business man then resident in London. He was noted for philanthropy and for a sustained interest in the more needy sections of the people. His son Mr. A. Cameron Corbett, M.P., became the first Lord Rowallan and presented Rouken Glen and other substantial properties to the City of Glasgow.

Soon the accommodation at Renfrew Lane was overtaxed and an additional Home, set apart for girls, was found nearby at 93 Renfield Street. All this meant more work, more planning, and more helpers. Every requirement was met day by day and, in addition to feeding, clothing and housing the little ones, some primary education was given.

Still the needy came, not only from Glasgow now, but from much further afield. It became known that this was a work for Scotland and children were welcomed from all parts of the country. To many Mr. Quarrier's Homes were a Godsend and not a few ministers are noted in the records as having brought orphans almost straight from a mother's death-bed, the mother's passing having been made easier by the knowledge that her children were not to be left without help and love.

The available accommodation could not cope and in 1872 a large mansion house at Cessnock, Govan, was bought for the lads and soon thereafter two Homes purchased for the girls, Newstead and Elmpark, in Govan Road. The Homes at Renfrew Lane and Renfield Street were eventually given up and work was concentrated at Cessnock and Govan Road for children, and at Dovehill, then later James Morrison Street, for mission enterprise and central administration.

The work at Cessnock was to continue for thirteen years until it, too, became part of the growing scene at Bridge of Weir. In his 'Narrative' for 1885, on 12th May, Mr. Quarrier writes :

> Today we have vacated old Cessnock Home on the Govan Road in which so many years of happy service for the Master have been spent. The house is very dilapidated, and the ground has been acquired by the Clyde Trust for their new docks, so that we could not remain longer, but God in His goodness has given us another 'Cessnock' in one of the Cottages at Bridge of Weir. Our mind goes back over the years that are past, and as we think of the hundreds of little ones who have been sheltered beneath its roof and taught of Jesus and His love, our hearts go out to God in praise and thanksgiving to Him for the countless blessings and privileges He has conferred upon us.

Whilst he laboured hard in the great city Quarrier saw visions in the night, and had dreams even in the daytime, of a children's village, set in pleasant farmland through which a burn would meander.

In the 1875 'Narrative' he puts it thus :

> The plan contemplated for the Cottage Homes is to buy or feu from 10 to 20 acres of land near Glasgow, and to build thereon 10 cottages to house 300 children, with schoolroom and workshops accommodation, each cottage to accommodate from 20 to 30 children, with a man and his wife to act as father and mother at the head of each household, with playground and other appliances attached to each cottage, and with a school-room in the centre; also, general workshops and small farm to be worked by the boys; the father of each family to be able to teach a different trade, such as tailor, shoemaker, joiner, baker, farmer, printer, smith, etc., the mother to do the work of each household with the assistance of the children . . . girls to be taught the usual household duties. The children would all meet together at school and church and on special occasions on the common playground, but at other times in their own playground. It is desirable to keep up the family and home feeling among children, and we believe this cannot be done so well in institutions where hundreds

are ruled by the uniform law necessary to keep large numbers in order who are housed together for years. Boys ready to go to trades in the city would be kept in a house there, presided over by a father and mother in the same way as in the Cottage Homes, till they are able to maintain themselves and begin the world on their own account. The first qualification necessary in the father and mother would be their fitness to train up the children in the 'nurture and admonition of the Lord'; and, second, their ability to understand the character of children, so as to maintain their respective individuality. The sum needed for purchasing land and building the cottages will be about £20,000. This is a large amount, but not too large for our Heavenly Father to send. . . . The buildings will be put under Trustees and all done in a business-like way. £1,000 will build a cottage capable of accommodating 20 to 30 children. What we require for the maintenance of the Homes will come as we need it. During the last four years all that we have wanted for feeding, clothing and educating the 320 children taken into the Homes has been sent in answer to prayer, and this leads us to trust in Him who has said :

'For your Heavenly Father knoweth that ye have need of all these things!'

All was to come true and, in time, a children's village, surpassing even the Founder's highest hopes was to be established in the midst of some of Scotland's fairest meadows.

A number of sites were looked at. Then early in April 1876 the farm of Nittingshill, in the Parish of Kilmacolm, Renfrewshire, came on the market. Mr. Quarrier bought the forty acres for £3,560. He now had land for his children's community and, no doubt to his delight, the waters of the Gryffe and the Catty formed its natural boundary. And the burn was there too! The site is a lovely one. There is woodland, undulating pastures, open prospects to north and south and, always in the distance, the hills, without which no Scot ever feels at home.

Now the friend of Scotland's children becomes architect, builder, civil engineer, Clerk of Works, sewage consultant, all rolled into one. Impatient to see the village take shape he

D

urges the designers and workmen on and, doubtless in
jubilant mood, records the laying of the first stone on 10th
February 1877, 'amidst much that was pleasing'.

During the whole of 1877 and into 1878 the work of
building went on apace. Mr. Quarrier's grand plan envisaged
a large Central Building which would house a hall, school-
room, offices, workshops and some staff accommodation.
Around this centre would be grouped ten cottages. The
cottages planned were spacious, solidly built, and conveniently
designed for the large families they would have to accommodate. Amazing as it may seem today such a house containing
something like ten rooms, could be built then for £1,300. The
money to put up two such homes came in almost right away
in single gifts and work was started on them. Cash had been
gathering for the project and this was used to begin the
Central Building but, when the trenches were dug, some
£1,500 were still needed to clear the cost.

On 2nd May 1878 Mr. and Mrs. Quarrier set sail for
Canada. They were looking forward to visiting many of the
children who had gone there, over the years, from the Homes.
They went with easy minds since only two days previously
all the money required for the first three buildings at Bridge
of Weir had been forthcoming.

When they returned to Scotland on 15th July the work was
well advanced and on 17th September in the midst of many
well-wishers the Revd. Dr. J. Marshall Lang, Minister of the
Barony Church, Glasgow, dedicated the buildings, which were
then formally opened. Despite bad weather conditions it was
a great day for William Quarrier; 'a day not to be forgotten
while memory lasts'.

The storms of the day damaged part of the roof of the
Central Building but did not prevent the attendance of men
and women from all over Scotland. The new hall was over-
crowded and many stood outside. They would not hear Mr.
Quarrier's moving words on that occasion. It is good to recall
what he then said :

I am here to testify that God has not failed me at any time. With regard to the present, I expect these Homes, with the ground, to be opened free of debt. As to the future, we have under our care about 180 children and young people. For ten months I never had more than a week's provision on hand, but as the day has come, so has the provision. All our assistance is due to the love which God puts into the hearts of His people, and I believe it will be the same to the end – 'the Lord will provide.' During the last seven years we have rescued 700 children, of whom 400 are in Canada. Of all the money entrusted to my hands only 5 per cent has been spent in helpers and servants. That is a fact which I commend to the consideration of business men. Whether I have to increase my expenditure I don't know, but, depend upon it, it will not be increased in the way of official payments.

A luncheon followed and, amongst others who spoke, was Dr. Barnardo, already deeply committed to similar work in England. In the evening the Lord Provost of Glasgow presided at a Grand Soirée. The day's proceedings got good press coverage and the following is quoted from the *North British Daily Mail* of 18th September :

It must have been with the liveliest satisfaction that Mr. Quarrier opened his Orphan Cottage Homes at Bridge of Weir yesterday. These Homes, costing £13,000, are the substantial outcome of many years of steady plodding, and they place the unmistakable mark of success upon the work in which he has been engaged. When Mr. Quarrier first began to devote himself to the rescuing of the gutter children by the establishment of a Shoeblack Brigade, some fourteen years ago, there was no special reason why he, of all men in Glasgow, should undertake the work. There are many men with greater leisure, and with ampler means, to whose hands such a work might seem to be more kindly than to a young tradesman in a modest way of business, who, having only got the ball of trade-success fairly at his foot, might have been excused for concentrating all his energies upon his own advancement during, at any rate, the best years of his life. . . .

And what has been done (in those years) by the agencies thus quietly set on foot? During the first seven years many hundreds of poor boys were helped to permanent situations who would otherwise have been destitute, or who would have lapsed into crime; and during the last seven years, seven hundred young people have been rescued from the gutters, and fairly started upon honest and useful lives. Properties have been purchased in the city and near Govan, and converted into training schools for the young Arabs of both sexes, and a number of the youngsters have had a complete outfit supplied to them and their passage paid to the Colonies, where they are now well-off and happy. . . . For a long time past he has had, on an average, a family of 200 helpless young people looking to him for daily bread, and during the last eight months he has never had above a week's supply of provisions in his store. . . . That over a thousand of such children should have been successfully laid hold of by one who was invested with no legal authority, but could use only persuasion, is matter of much astonishment, and gives Mr. Quarrier a strong claim upon the confidence of the public . . . after everyone else has got his due, the fact remains that to Mr. Quarrier belongs the credit of having, to all intents and purposes, made the only practical attempt to grapple with and successfully solve the great social problem of what to do with our gutter children.

1878 saw the failure of the City of Glasgow Bank and this gave Mr. Quarrier some anxiety since a number of those who had supported his work in the past were financially crippled. The Homes' Building Fund money was also lodged with the Bank and the suspension of business held up payment of several accounts. However, in the end all worked out well and Quarrier's prayers for his children and their needs were all answered.

The village continued to expand and the demand for accommodation did not slacken. By 1888 twenty cottages had been built and, alongside the houses, a laundry, workshops, bakehouse, and 'Homelea', where the Founder and his family lived. In addition a splendid Church had been erected for the children and staff. Built in the Gothic style, and with seating for 1,000 people, the church was opened on 6th March 1888. Its 120-feet-high tower remains a prominent landmark over a wide area. Its clock marks the passing hours and its bells ring out their melodious tunes to delight the ear and to call to worship. Their sound remains in the mind of many a Quarrier's child over the years and letters from 'old' boys and girls often tell how a well-loved Psalm tune, or a fine peal,

heard in some distant land, immediately brings back memories
of the home of their youth. Later the church was enlarged
and today it can seat some 2,000 worshippers. From its
pulpit many a notable preacher has told the story of Jesus,
and no one can tell the number of young folk who have given
Him their allegiance within its walls.

The future of the young villagers was not overlooked. In
addition to apprenticeship schemes, house work was taught
both sexes. As was fitting in an island people quite a number
of boys wished to go to sea and, in order to advance their
training, a ship, the *James Arthur*, was set up on the river
banks and 'launched' on 1st March 1888.

Children need education, they also fall sick from time to
time. In 1892 the Homes School was opened and the 'Narrative' for that year also lists 'Elim' Home for incurably sick
boys and 'Bethesda' Home for sick girls. The figures for
that year, the twenty-first of Mr. Quarrier's work for children,
are an indication of the scope of his activity. The year began
with 731 children at Bridge of Weir; 454 new children were
admitted from the City Home in Glasgow, making a total of
1,185. These were looked after and distributed as follows:
Sent to Canada 249; sent to City Home 9; to other institutions
2; to sea 3; adopted 3; died 16; returned to friends 55; left
3; dismissed 2; leaving 843 at Bridge of Weir on 31st
October 1892. In addition, 669 'homeless, friendless wan-
derers' had been provided with a night's shelter in various
model lodging houses in Glasgow. Mr. Quarrier had also
obtained 'lines'* for thirty-five sick and delicate boys and
girls which enabled them to be looked after in hospitals and
Convalescent Homes. He also records concerning Glasgow,
'over 200 evangelistic meetings held in our own halls . . . and
many visits paid to the poor of the district by our missionary
and voluntary workers'.

All this demanded a great deal of money and Quarrier still
stood by his oft-repeated principle 'We never call on anyone

* A recommendation, usually given by a subscriber to an Institution,
stating that the holder is suitable for, and worthy of, admission.

for money, nor do we send out collectors, nor go out to give lectures to get money, or resort to bazaars or entertainments for the purpose of raising it. The work is the Lord's and we commit *everything* to Him in prayer, believing that He will supply, through His children, what we require.' At the end of 1892 it is recorded yet again that this simple faith is justified. During the year £11,615 6s. 6d. had been given for work amongst the children and £4,053 13s. 1d. towards the Homes' Building Fund. The year ended with £1,250 11s. 1¾d. in hand for the children's needs and a total of £19,464 9s. 8¼d. in the Building Fund. At this time it was costing some £40 a day to keep the enterprise going, a considerable sum of money then. Yet the need was always met. Well might Quarrier record 'the work of the Homes from the first until now has, we believe, been a standing rebuke to the sceptic who denies that there is a God, or One who hears and answers the prayers of His children'.

Naturally, Mr. Quarrier had his critics. Was he not going too far? Was his pace not too fast? Would the public goodwill last? Could one expect the initial momentum to be maintained? To all such queries William Quarrier had the same answer. The need was there and did not diminish. As long as it existed, and as long as the Lord provided, the work would expand. And expand it did. By the time Quarrier died in 1903 the Orphan Homes and Sanatoria at Bridge of Weir comprised some 64 buildings and 1,526 children were in care. In addition there were the City Orphan Home in Glasgow; 'Fairknowe' at Brockville, Ontario, Canada; and 'Benthead' Seaside Home, Ardnadam.

Tuberculosis Sanatoria

At first sight it appears strange that this busy man, so completely dedicated to children, almost without any leisure, should take in hand the building of Scotland's first Tuberculosis Sanatorium. When, however, one reads his Diaries of Admission the reason for this new venture becomes clear. Page after page tells of parents dying from the dread consumption. This was the disease which so often produced orphans. Quarrier believed in prevention rather than cure and, inevitably, his restless and probing mind turned towards ways and means of preventing this scourge and, where this was impossible, of halting the illness. He quickly realised that, if one had the money, the illness could be treated and some relief secured from hospital treatment in a favourable climate. He determined to make as good provision as possible in Scotland for the afflicted poor. His ambition was neatly phrased by one of his contemporaries, Sir Charles Cameron, who wrote that Mr. Quarrier's aim on behalf of those who were without the means to help themselves was 'to establish for them a Riviera in Renfrewshire, to provide for Lazarus the pure air, warmth, nourishment, and comfort hitherto monopolised by Dives, and to secure for them the best and most careful nourishment and treatment that medicine and nursing could devise'. He was spurred on in his endeavour by the incidence of the disease amongst his orphan children. For their sake, as well as for the sake of the older generation, he determined that something had to be done. In characteristic manner he went to see what was already being attempted at Ventnor, Isle of Wight, and at Brompton in London, and made himself familiar with all aspects of the sickness and its treatment. He consulted with doctors and leading medical men and then, in his 'Narrative' for 1893, he makes public his intention to proceed with a sanatorium. The building he envisaged, fully equipped, would cost £7,500. On 29th December he was confirmed in his decision to go ahead with the scheme when friends in the east of Scotland said they would meet the whole cost. The following month three donations of £1,000 each came in and another £3,730 in smaller sums, 'from £100 down to the widow's mite of 5s. and the little girl's saved pennies.'

The farm of Carsemeadow adjoins Nittingshill on which the children's village had been built. Eminently suitable as a sanatorium site, it was also on the market. It was bought for £6,722 and the hospital's foundation stone was laid on 5th

September 1894. The Sanatorium and the Executive Building were opened by Lady Glen Coats on 3rd September 1896. Drainage problems delayed admissions but on 27th May 1898 the first patient was received and by the end of October that year there were thirty-one.

Six leading doctors acted as an Advisory Board and gave guidance in all medical matters. They aided and encouraged Quarrier further in this part of his work by issuing a public statement giving their reasons for supporting him.

Here, again, the need was greater than the provision made and on 5th September 1900 a second Sanatorium was opened at a cost of £10,000. A third was added in 1904. The following years saw various additions until the Bridge of Weir Hospital for Consumptives became not only the first, but also the largest, in Scotland. Its equipment has always been up-to-date and its doctors and nurses have been skilled and attentive. Many have been restored to health because of it and, had Quarrier done nothing other than this, his name would have been deservedly honoured.

Under the provisions of the new National Health Service Scheme the whole Sanatoria was transferred to the State on 5th July 1948 and came under the management of the Secretary of State for Scotland as part of the Western Regional Hospitals Board. From its beginnings until then eleven thousand, four hundred and fifty patients had been cared for. At the time of transfer the buildings alone were valued at £180,000. These, along with the grounds, the furnishings and fittings, and considerable financial assets, were taken over by the State without any recompense. With the great advances in medicine seen in recent years Tuberculosis is no longer a scourge, and mercifully there are few such patients now in the Hospital. It continues to serve the area, however, and to play an important part in the Western Region's care of the sick.

Colony of Mercy

In 1901 Mr. Quarrier was 72 years of age. He had worked unceasingly. He had planned continuously. He had done more than a man's job. Yet, still he saw work to be done, and his compassionate heart was stirred. That year he wrote :

> For many years it has been in our hearts that some provision should be made in Scotland for relieving the lot of the sane Epileptics, but the claims of the extending Homes and Sanatoria have hindered us from taking any steps in the matter. A friend having recently offered us some financial assistance, we feel that God is directing us to bring the needs of this affected class before His Stewards with a view to the establishment of a Colony somewhat on the same lines as that carried out so successfully by Pastor Von Bodelschwingh at Bielefield, in Germany, and by others in America. To gain information regarding the English Institution, when in London attending the Congress on Tuberculosis, we visited the Chalfont Saint Peter Colony for Epileptics in Buckinghamshire. We also visited the Maghull Home for Epileptics, near Liverpool, established twelve years ago.
>
> Scotland is behind other civilised nations in having no place but the poorhouse and asylum for such afflicted ones, and as it is computed that there are 4000 in Scotland alone, there is need that something be done to ameliorate their condition. . . . The calls of those sorely stricken ones should call forth universal sympathy, and we hope to see the day when Scotland will have a Colony of Mercy, national in its character, and dominated by the Spirit of our Lord and Master Who on earth said of such, 'Bring him to me.'

Mr. Quarrier did not live to see the Colony of Mercy for which he pleaded. He did, however, make its presence possible. He planned to build on some 200 acres of land. Here would be erected two houses for men, two for women, and one each for boys and girls. He reckoned he would need £20,000 to bring this about. Good donations were forth-coming and in May 1903, just a few months before his death, he bought the farm of Hatrick alongside the Orphan Homes and Sanatoria, for the sum of £9,800. It extends to 213 acres, has a good outlook, and is in every sense the right place for such a Colony. Within a year of Quarrier's death his daughter, Mary, laid the foundation stone of the first building, and on 26th September 1906 the first Home was opened by Lord

Maclay. The story of its development falls naturally into a later chapter. Even in his last months on earth the old warrior's compassion was matched by a youthful zest to experiment.

Canada

It will be remembered that from the beginning William Quarrier envisaged an Emigration Scheme as part of his service to the needy children who were brought to him, or whom he found. To begin with he organised this in association with Miss Annie Macpherson who, working from London, had set up three Receiving Homes in Canada. One such home was Knowlton, Quebec; another Belleville on Lake Ontario, and the third at Galt, Ontario. The name of this third Home was 'Blair Athole'. It was a ten-roomed house set in ninety-nine acres of rich farmland and here a number of the young Scots were trained in domestic and farm work. From 'Blair Athole' and the other two Homes many children were adopted by Canadian families and given a new hope and a new life. The others were trained, loved, and provided for, until they, too, having reached working age, went out to face the world, well equipped for the adventure and opportunity of emergent Canada.

Quarrier wasted no time in putting his plans into operation and on 2nd July 1872, less than eight months after setting up the first Home in Renfrew Lane, a party of thirty-five children set sail for Quebec on board the s.s. *St. David*. It cost only £10 to equip and convey each child to Canada! Mr. Quarrier kept his various accounts apart and the £350 necessary for this party had all been forthcoming, clearly marked for this purpose.

This part of his work brought a measure of criticism. Was he not depleting the labour market at home? Was he not encouraging the separation of young lives from such friends as they might have in Scotland? Was it really a good idea to ship to a land, just beginning to grow, so many children whose memories were bound to be affected by the hardships they had known? People airing such views just did not know the type of child Quarrier was helping. Had they done so they would have rejoiced in the great change for the better being offered each one. Canadians themselves were to acknowledge, with gratitude, the good that was done their country through Mr. Quarrier's work. In the main the young Scots proved good stock, who served well the country of their adoption.

Mr. Quarrier's own attitude to this part of his work is clearly put in his first 'Narrative' of 1872:

> By the emigration feature of the work we are enabled to place these children in Christian homes in Canada, where they will be kindly cared for and watched over by Miss Macpherson and her helpers. By this means we hope to be enabled yearly to rescue a fresh set of boys and girls, whilst, without this providential outlet, we should be stocked up with the same set of children for four or five years, and unable to rescue more. And to those who object to emigration as withdrawing labour from this country, we would say, 'Come and see the children as we take them in, and you will perceive that not the labour market, but the crime market, is likely to be affected by our work of rescue.'

For a quarter of a century band after band of young folk from the Orphan Homes followed the first thirty-five. By the end of 1897 no fewer than two thousand, six hundred and eighty-eight of the boys and girls who had been rescued by Quarrier were fitted out and taken across to new homes in the West. Quarrier himself paid a number of visits to Canada and personally supervised the overall programme. In 1887 he purchased his own Canadian Home and receiving centre, 'Fairknowe' at Brockville, Ontario. His daughter and son-in-law, Mr. and Mrs. A. Burges, crossed the Atlantic and took charge of it. Over the years the Quarrier family, now growing up, became responsible citizens and were well thought of. Alas!, however, in 1897, trouble was encountered. It is not necessary to go over the whole sad episode. Suffice it to say that certain sectional interests in Canada took alarm at the number of children entering the country under such schemes as Quarrier organised. The Government of Ontario was persuaded to pass an 'Act to regulate the Immigration into Ontario of Certain Classes of Children'. The provisions of the Act really meant that those children were, in some degree, 'marked'. They were to be placed under official control from the time they entered the country until their eighteenth birthday. A licence had to be taken out by each Distributing Home. An account of each child's background had to be produced and the account had to be kept up-to-date regarding character, habits, and so on, during the formative years. If such a child had a job and lost it, or changed to another, all the reasons had to be entered. In other words, a file, or dossier, was to be available for each child in the classified category. Some of this might have been necessary, even good, but Quarrier felt that since such regulations were applied only to children such as he brought into Canada, it amounted to unjust treatment. Let such a requirement be laid upon every immigrant child and he would co-operate. But if this Act applied only to those little ones whom life had already treated harshly, and who had no champion but God and those whom He had called to care for them, then co-operate Quarrier would not. He was in Canada at this time and had conversations with the Premier and other members of the Ontario Legislature. They had nothing but praise for his work and for the children he had sent. Why then the Act? Quarrier could get no answer that satisfied his sense of justice and he determined to halt his Emigration Scheme the moment this Act became law. The Legislature passed the Act in 1897 and immediately the doughty William ceased to send any child under eighteen years of age to Canada. In the event it is likely that both Canada and the children suffered. Yet one cannot do other than admire the champion who stood up for justice as he saw it, and spoke up for those little ones who had no one else on earth but William Quarrier to fight their battle. It is certain that respect for his charges forced him to act as he did.

During those 25 years the smallest annual contingent to go to Canada numbered eighteen, in 1879. The highest number to go in any one year was a band of two hundred and sixty-eight, who sailed the seas in 1893.

Although after 1897 the scheme was officialy at an end, a few children continued to make the journey to Canada to join brothers and sisters. Some others, over eighteen years of age, also made the trip.

When Mr. Quarrier died it was decided to look into the question once more. After consultation and visits emigration began again in 1904 and continued until 1932. The period immediately thereafter was one of world-wide depression and Canada suffered in the general malaise. Immigration was not then encouraged by any Government. In 1934 'Fairknowe' was sold. However, in 1938, some twenty-eight children from the Orphan Homes went to the Dominion. The following year the Second World War was upon mankind. After the war, social conditions had changed enormously, and the emigration part of the work ended, although, from time to time, small parties have gone to Australia.

We have travelled far from the small beginnings in Renfrew Lane. The poor, ragged and hesitant Andrew, who crept in for shelter on November 18th 1871, is foremost in an army of thousands of waifs, strays, unwanted and unfortunate children, whom William Quarrier took to his heart in the name of Jesus of Nazareth. Although 6,687 went to Canada, many more remained at home and were trained to work and live as decent, law-abiding citizens, inheriting in the home-land a life splendid beyond their early dreams.

> Bring me your poor, your needy, your neglected;
> Bring me your sick, sad and suffering ones;
> Bring me your afflicted and greatly burdened.

This was the plea and command of William Quarrier.

They were brought to him, or found by him. In Cottage Home, in Classroom, in Hospital ward and in Christian sanctuary, he clothed, fed, loved and healed them. And all

was made possible through one man who was brave enough
to take God at His Word. Together Mr. Quarrier and his
many charges might well quote the words of the Psalmist :

'They looked unto Him and were lightened and their faces were
not ashamed.'

(Ps. 34 v. 5)

CHAPTER 6

What Manner of Man?

IT is one of the mysteries of life that the camera, the tape-recorder, and television were not with man from the beginning! What would the world not give to be able to see and hear Jesus of Nazareth; St. Paul in the midst of his missionary journeys; Christopher Columbus venturing towards the Americas; Martin Luther heralding the Reformation; Abraham Lincoln at Gettysburg? What would Scotland not give to be able to hear and see St. Ninian at Whithorn; St. Columba, carrying the Gospel from Iona to the Northern Picts; a dialogue between Mary, Queen of Scots and John Knox; the clash of Battle at Bannockburn; James Watt watching his kettle; the agony of the Highland Clearances; the daring of Bonnie Prince Charlie, and much else renowned in our story? Those who have followed this tale so far may indeed wish that the hearing and seeing were possible in the case of William Quarrier. Such a spirit deserves to be known. Such a work as he accomplished ought to have a permanent and vivid record.

Fortunately, the camera was here in his time and we can see him. His photographs show a well-built man, somewhat austere, perhaps, yet with a kind light in his eyes. He has a compelling face, strong and rugged in the Scottish fashion. His hands are large and look accustomed to work, as indeed they were. The impression given is one of capability and strength of will. It is the face of a single-minded man who, if he had not been refined by the grace of God, might well have become ruthless. At the same time, there is always the suggestion of a smile, and it must have been that suggestion, along with the look in his eye, that brought little children to him and kept them there.

But there was no tape-recorder so we cannot hear his voice. George Müller of Bristol and Dr. Barnardo of London, his colleagues in child care, preached much. Apart from Services at the Homes' Church William Quarrier did not do so. He did not claim any ability in the pulpit, although on the public platform, his utter sincerity and clarity of expression were extremely telling. Probably he was at his speaking best when he told his children the story of the love of Christ, and of his own faith. Indeed, the children could not but be impressed since the divine response to that faith breathed in every stone in their village.

The surest way of getting to know the man, however, is through his written word. Although there exists in the Bridge of Weir archives only one letter that can be identified as his, there is, fortunately, a complete record of his work from the beginning right up to his death, in the annual Narratives which he wrote and had printed. These are beautifully bound, meticulously detailed and movingly written. Within their pages, history, personal tragedy, comedy, hope, compassion, all mingle, and almost always, a little child is at the centre. In addition, a number of manuscript Diaries are extant. Although they are mainly records of admission and discharge, much else has been added and they make fascinating reading. One cannot be certain that they were written by Quarrier in whole or, even, in part. Yet the spirit is his. Taken together with the Narratives we have a splendid library of Scotland's social condition during Quarrier's lifetime. We have, also, a first-class picture of the man's vision and concern. Let the diaries speak for themselves and tell of the children's friend.

SUDDEN CALL

Wednesday May 17th 1876

I was asked today to attend the funeral of Jessie G., a domestic servant, 24 years of age, who left her Highland

The Colony Entrance

Cottage No. 10

home on Saturday morning both strong and healthful; to spend a day or two with an acquaintance resident in Glasgow before going to her new place. On Saturday night Jessie was out purchasing some little things she stood in need of and was then quite happy. About 3 o'clock on Sabbath morning she became very ill with obstruction of the bowels. The doctor was sent for who did everything in his power to save her life, but every attempt proved fruitless. Her journey was drawing to a close, and after twenty-six hours' suffering Jessie, in the bloom of youth and womanhood, was taken to her rest, 'That rest which alone remaineth for the people of God'. Truly, she was away from her own kindred, in a strange land, and amongst strange people, and buried by strangers.

By wire her friends, immediately after death, were appraised of the sad event that had fallen upon them. Her mother and sister came here on Tuesday morning and her brother was to have been this morning but, as fate would have it, he met with an accident which deprived him of seeing the dead body of his sister or of his following her remains to their last resting-place. When asked if she had any fear of death she said, 'How can I fear when at the foot of the cross?' Then, 'Lift me up' she cried 'higher . . . up to heaven'; after which she uttered the last words she ever breathed: 'Come quickly!'

OF SUCH IS THE KINGDOM

March 24th 1880

James, Jane and Hannah R. Father died of typhus fever in Belvedere and mother was in the Royal Infirmary when Jane (eldest daughter) took the fever on 3rd December., and was taken to the hospital. The mother, against the doctor's orders, left the Infirmary and went to keep the family together. The father and children, about the same time, all took fever and were removed to the Belvedere Hospital, where the father died on the 1st January. The children, after getting better, came home to find their mother was in the last stages of consumption, of which she

E

died. The children were today turned out of their home at
79 Cadogan Street by the landlord who seized and sold the
few sticks of furniture, turning the children out on the
street.

At the end of this entry is added 'The above James R.
died of consumption on 21st March 1883 and was buried on
the 24th inst. in Kilmacolm churchyard. 7/6/84 Janie and
Hannah to Canada.'

1882

William J., 12 yrs. 5 Jan. next. The illegitimate son of
E.H., . . . Carlisle, who has had six children for different
fathers. She has been a most infamous character and kept a
house of ill fame. Mrs. Currie, in course of her house to
house visitation, met in with her, and both mother and son
have been going to Salvation Army meetings. Another boy
at home earning 3s. weekly. Although William has attended
school regularly he is very dull and slow and only in 1st
Book. Mrs. C. called on 6th July to enquire about the case.
Came to Nittingshill O.H.S. 21st August 1882 and placed
in No. 9 Cottage. Education – 1st Book.

A footnote says 'Removed from there to his mother 4th
Feb. 1885'.

Wednesday, June 14th 1876

James N. has gone today on board the Mary Goodell for a
twelve months' voyage to St. Lawrence and from thence to
Melbourne and then home, for £2 per month; E. M. Amos,
Master.

This was one of the trickiest boys in the Home. The other
morning he had the big toe of each boy in the room tied to
the bed, and next morning their noses were all painted red.
Amongst the boys he went under the name of Priest. His
father and mother are both dead. He was in a fearful state
of filth when we got him. We had to burn his clothes and rig
him out anew.

FRAE A' THE AIRTS...

Monday, August 21st 1876

Sophia S. 22 years of age. This girl came here from Constantinople. Was serving with Mrs. Christie, Missionary to the Jews, who gives her a good character.

THE LABOURER IS WORTHY OF HIS HIRE...

15th April 1882

John and James D., 10 and 8 years. Father was a store-keeper with O., Cheesemongers in Candleriggs, and only receiving 22s. weekly.

HOW MUCH?

24th May 1882

Thomas P., 10 yrs. in August. Has been lodged with a Mr. T., Thistle Street, since he was a child and paid regularly each half year, but now says £5 can't keep him and would require £7 (per annum). T's wife died two years ago and since that time the boy has been allowed to run about as he liked. . . . Came to Nittingshill 24th May 1882. Education neglected.

THE EDINBURGH REVIEW

September 29th 1881

William C., 9 yrs. on 20th Sept., Isabella C., 7 yrs. on 13th Aug., Elizabeth C., 5 yrs. on 4th June.

Father was Sergt. of Police in Central Division, and was found dead on his own stair at 2.30 a.m. by Volunteers returning from Review at Edinburgh on 26th August 1881. His time was not up till 5-a.m. but it is presumed he had been making his way home, not feeling well, when he dropped down. He was a big stout man and disease of the heart is given as the cause of his untimely death. The mother died at Christmas two years ago.

It is added that Isabella and William went to Canada on

7th June 1884 and that Elizabeth died at the Homes on 1st April 1885.

WHAT A CHILD MAY BRING . . .

1882

Marion McM., 13 on 19th July, Admitted 6th October 1882. The father of this illegitimate child has not been heard of since her birth. Mother was an invalid for five years prior to her death, which took place in May 1882. During her illness Marion was nurse. She had a very successful operation performed in Infirmary and was afterwards in Convalescent Home.

Mrs. Daly, 185 Hill Street, Govanhill, has been greatly interested in her and got her own Doctor to see her. He thinks good food etc. will bring her round. Mrs. Arthur, Bible Woman, 36 Willowbank Street, knew the mother for many years.

A title-deed for lair in Sighthill Cemetery is handed over with child.

Marion went from the Homes to service in August 1895.

WHAT'S IN A NAME? . . .

On 21st October 1882 it is recorded that William Ewart Gladstone McInally, 9¾ yrs. of age, was admitted at Nittingshill. (Diligent search has not shown the admission of any Winston Spencer Churchill MacTavish!)

ENTERPRISE IN CANADA

From the *Canadian Distribution Home Report* for 1886:

'Peter was a great source of amusement to all on board the *Buenos Ayrean* rather resembling Sir Roger Tichborne in his size. His great anxiety to sing came somewhat in conflict with his shortness of breath, so that the rendering of his childish piece, "Two Little Eyes", was generally received with hearty laughter, at which he complacently looked round in wonder. One afternoon a farmer and his wife called wanting a boy to assist them in light "chores". A number were brought into the parlour for selection – among them Master Peter; he scanned the couple carefully, and after singing was over, he climbed the man's knee, put his arms round his neck and whispered "Dada" – this was irresistible and quickly won their hearts : the older boys were dismissed and little Peter reigns alone in his new Canadian home.'

These extracts tell something of the spirit Quarrier brought to his work and of his place in the social structure of his age. But more must be said. One cannot but be amazed at his advanced ideas in the realm of child welfare. In a day when most people thought of large institutions as being adequate for the deprived child, Quarrier saw how unsatisfactory these were and planned small cottage homes for them. It has to be admitted that the demand meant that some thirty children had to be accommodated in each cottage, far too great a number we should say today. Yet, what an advance that was in the 19th century! And how noble his concept of the children's village. Away from slums, and greyness, apart from street-corner temptation and exploitation, his children would have the best of the good earth and air and sky. With good house parents, steady education and, always, the knowledge of Christ, their spirits, their minds, and their bodies, would grow in strength and beauty.

Quarrier had, of course, his defects. There is no doubt that he was an autocrat of the Victorian school. Not for him the democratic rule of Committees and Councils! His first experience of such was when he set up his Brigades in Glasgow. Soon he realised that to get anything done he simply had to forge ahead on his own. This suited him, in any case, and it was his way to the end. Yet he did not despise help. Indeed he was fortunate in the many influential men and women of his time who came to his aid and, when necessary, he consulted with them. Nevertheless he was always the Brigadier-General and the decisions were his.

He was also dour. At one time he was in dispute with Renfrew County Council about the payment of rates. For

sixteen years these had not been demanded, the County
Council being able to exempt the Homes from payment under
the provisions of the 1869 'Sunday and Ragged School Act'.
In return Quarrier made no demand on the services of the
County in any way. Local policy, however, changed, and he
was asked to pay a considerable sum, and then to meet the
annual burden. He took his case for exemption to the Court
of Session, but to no avail. It is said he then marched his
thousand children to the nearest County School and virtually
said 'All right, I pay. Now you educate!' It is an old story and,
in the end, an amicable settlement was reached. But the
dourness of the man is seen. So also is his inborn sense of
fairplay and justice.

One is tempted to wonder how much William Quarrier
was influenced in his work by George Müller of Bristol.
Perhaps they met during Müller's preaching tours in Scotland
during 1875/76. Indeed this seems almost certain since
Müller was in Glasgow for a single visit of thirty-six days
in 1875. He had many meetings and preached in various
churches. Quarrier is almost bound to have made contact
with him then. That some influence was present is undoubted,
since Quarrier copied the other man's title for his annual
Report, 'A Narrative of Facts.' Yet Quarrier's actual planning
was quite different.

Barnardo and Quarrier began at practically the same time
and we have seen that Dr. Barnardo was present at the
opening of the first Bridge of Weir buildings. There is no
record of any further contact but one would imagine that the
doctor in London and the shoemaker at Bridge of Weir
would continue to learn of each other and to profit from their
growing experience. Certainly Miss Macpherson with her
Emigration Scheme would be a continuing link.

It is sometimes asked 'What would Quarrier do today?'
In many ways this is a fruitless question. The times are
vastly different and Quarrier himself would be a product of our
own age. One thing is sure. His questing, consecrated, spirit
would continually search out new ways of helping the needy.

Perhaps today he would be drawn to the loneliness of the aged. Certainly the epileptics' continuing need of understanding and love, as well as medical treatment, would claim his attention. There is no doubt the violence of the age would lead him to preventive work in this field, and he might well organise training schools and courses for boys and girls having their first casual brush with authority. Although the needs of children are other than in his lifetime he would still be their champion and friend.

Above all, William Quarrier was a man of faith. When all else is said and done this is what comes out of his story. He claimed the response of God to the needs of children, in the name of the One who said: 'Suffer the little children to come unto me, and forbid them not. . . .' Today we tend to be wary of such a simple trust. Yet that simple trust was wonderfully answered in Quarrier's own day, and has continued to be answered, in respect of the Homes he founded, for a hundred years. It is this signal fact that remains in the mind. Time and again one is brought back to its challenge and significance. If it works here why not elsewhere? Perhaps the answer is that there are not enough Quarriers!

Once, towards the end of his life, he lay ill. He had promised to write an article for *The Sunday Magazine* on 'Answers to Prayer'. He was too weak to do so and a reporter visited his bedside and took down in shorthand what he had to say. In February 1897 the article was published.

Here is the authentic William Quarrier:

ANSWERS TO PRAYER

For twenty-five years it has been with me a continual answer to prayer. The first seven of my service were spent in caring for the rough boys of the streets of Glasgow, but having made a vow, when I was very young, that if God prospered me I should build houses for orphans, I was not satisfied with that work among the bigger boys. Being in business, however, and having a family to maintain, the question of whether I could do more was a difficult one. I was giving eight hours a day to the work, and in the Shoe-Black Brigade, the Parcels Brigade, and the Newspaper

Brigade had probably about three hundred boys to care for. While I considered what could be done, a lady – Miss Macpherson – from London called, and in the course of our talk about the little ones, she urged that I should attempt something more than I was doing. For three months I prayed to God for guidance, and in the end resolved that if He sent me £2,000, I should embark in the greater work. Nobody knew of that resolution; it was a matter between God and myself. If God wanted me to do more work than I was doing, I felt that He would send me the £2,000, not in proportions, but in a solid sum. I was then before the public, and I wrote a letter to the newspapers pleading that something more should be done for street children, pointing out that the Poorhouse and the Reformatory were not the best means of helping child-life, and urging that something on the Home or Family system was desirable. There was a strong conviction that God would answer the prayer, and, the terms of the prayer being explicit, I believed the answer would be unmistakable. After waiting thirteen days the answer came. Amongst my other letters was one from a Scotch friend in London, to the effect that the writer would, to the extent of £2,000, provide me with money to buy or rent a house for orphan children. When I received that call I felt that my family interests and my business interests should be second, and that God's work among the children should be first.

To a business man, it was a call to surrender what you would call business tact. I had to rise up there and then, and proclaim in the midst of the commercial city of Glasgow, that from that moment I was to live by faith, and depend on God for money, wisdom and strength. From that time forward I would ask no man for money, but trust God for everything. That £2,000 was the first direct answer to prayer for money. He gave me the utmost of my asking, and I felt that I would need to give Him the utmost of the power I pledged.

We rented a common workshop in Renfrew Lane — it was very difficult to get a suitable place – to lodge the children in, and that little place was the first National Home for Orphans in Scotland, and from which has sprung what the visitor may see today amongst the Renfrewshire hills. One day, I remember, two boys came in, and we had everything to clothe them with except a jacket for one of them. The matron, a very godly woman, said 'We must just pray that God will send what is needed,' and we prayed that He would. That night a large parcel of clothing came from Dumbarton, and in it was a jacket that fitted the boy as if it had been made for him. That was a small thing, of course, but if you don't see God in the gift of a pair of stockings, you won't see Him in a gift of £10,000.

We had thirty children in that Home, and we kept praying that the Lord would open a place for us somewhere in the country. A friend called on me and offered to sub-let Cessnock House, with three acres of ground about it. Cessnock Dock has now absorbed the place, and as it was just the very spot we wanted, we accepted. We had room for a hundred boys, and with the help of God we prospered. We had resolved formerly that we would send children to Canada, but it took £10 per head to send them, and we were determined not to get into debt. We had only a few pounds in hand when we took the house in Govan Road, and it took £200 to alter it. But every night we prayed that the Lord would send money to pay for the alterations. Sums varying from 5/- to £5 came in, but when the bills came to be paid we were short £100. A friend not far from one of my places of business sent for me, and when I called, he said 'How are you getting on at Cessnock?' I said we were getting on nicely, and that we had got £100 towards the alterations. He gave me £100, to my astonishment, for I knew that he could not afford so much, but he said a relative who died in England had left him a fortune, and the money was to help me in the work God had given me to do. In that answer you see how God works mysteriously to accomplish His purpose and help those who put their trust in Him.

God gives us great help in dealing with the wayward, wilful boys of the Home. They are generally lads who have known no control; but we are able, with God's blessing on our efforts, to get them to do almost anything that is wanted, without strap or confinement or threat. To hear boys who used to curse and swear praying to God, and to see them helping other boys in the Home, is to me the most encouraging feature of the work God has given me to do. Whilst I sought to clothe and educate them, I left God to deal with them in their spirits; and to-day the result of the spiritual work amongst the boys and girls of Glasgow exceeds anything I ever expected.

I still thought of the emigration scheme, and in 1872 we had sixty children that were able to go to Canada. Of course it meant £600 to send them, and we had the necessary money except £70 in the end of June. We prayed on that God would send the balance before the day of sailing, 2nd. July. A friend called at one of my places of business to see me, and subsequently I had an interview with him. He gave me £50, and said it was from one who did not wish the name mentioned. 'What shall I put it to?' I asked. 'Anything you like,' he said. 'We are short of £70 for the emigration of our first band of children to Canada, and if you like I shall put it to that.' 'Do so,' he said; and as the man left I saw God's hand in the gift that had been made. When I went home that night I found amongst my letters one in which was enclosed £10 'to take a child to Canada,' and the post on the following morning brought two five-pound notes from other friends, making up exactly at the moment it was needed the sum I had asked God to give.

In addition to the Homes, we carried on mission work amongst lapsed masses, and, as in the case of the Homes, we were firmly resolved to do everything by prayer and supplication. I rented an old church at the head of the Little Dovehill, just where the Board school stands now, as a hall, but we did not have the whole of it. At the level of the gallery another floor had been introduced, and while we occupied the upper flat, a soap manufacturer occupied the lower. In a way it was a trial of faith to go up those stairs past the soap work into our hall. We wanted to open the place free of debt, and the money for the alterations came in gradually. I remember putting it to the Lord to send a suitable evangelist if He wished the work to go on. At that time – twenty-four years ago – we heard a lot of Joshua Poole and his wife, who were having great blessing in London, and I thought that they were just the people to reach the working classes. But as I had convictions about women preaching – which by the way I have not now – I asked the Lord to send £50 to cover the expense for a month if it were His will that these friends should come to Glasgow and preach nightly during that period. I left it to God to decide whether we should ask these friends or not, and I had the assurance – the assurance of faith – that the money would come. When I went home that night I found that a friend had called at one of my places of business and left fifty one-pound notes without knowing my mind and without knowing I needed it. After that I felt that God was going to work a great work amongst the lapsed masses of Glasgow, and He did so; for six months we rented the Scotia Music Hall on Sabbath evenings, and instead of a month the evangelists were six in the city conducting services every night. When they left 10,000 people gathered on the Green to bid them farewell. Hundreds were led to the Saviour.

After a number of years' work in Glasgow with the Girls' Home, in Govan with the Boys' Home, and with the Mission premises, the need of a farm became great. I prayed for money to purchase a farm of about fifty acres, three miles or so from

Glasgow. It was to have a burn running through it, good drainage, and everything necessary. I was anxious to get this burn for the children to paddle in and fish in; but I feel now that at the time I was rebellious against God in fixing the site so near Glasgow. We visited a dozen places, but the cost was so great that I was fairly beaten. God had shut up every door.

A friend met me on the street, and asked if I had seen the farm in Kilmacolm Parish that was to be sold. I replied that I had not, and that I considered the place too far away. In talking over the matter, he persuaded me to go and see the farm, and when I did go, and standing where our big central building is now, saw that it had everything I prayed for – perfect drainage, and not only the burn, but a river and a large flat field for a recreation ground – I said in my heart to the Lord : 'This will do.' Ever since I have blessed the Lord for that; my way is not God's way, and so He shut us in amongst these Renfrewshire hills, away from the ways of men.

After paying £3,560 for the farm, we had about £1,500 left, and in 1887 we began to build a church and school, to cost £5,000. I told the contractor that we would stop if the money did not come in; but it kept coming in, and the work went on. In 1888 I had resolved to go to Canada, with the party of children going out that year, and I saw clearly that I would need to stop the contractors if I got no more money in the interval, for I was still £1,400 short. Yet I believed the Lord would send the money before I left in the latter end of May, though the time I write of was as far on as the middle of the month. I kept praying, and the assurance was strong that the money would come. Just three days before the date on which I was to sail, a friend came to me, and said it had been laid upon his heart to build one of the cottages at Bridge of Weir, but the Lord, he thought, would accept the money for the central building just as much as though it were put into houses, and he handed me £1,300.

All the money belonging to the Homes and all my own was in the City of Glasgow Bank when it failed, and hundreds of the givers were involved as well. On my way up from the Homes on the day of the disaster, a gentleman met me, and told me the sad news. At the moment I realised what the news meant for me – my own personal loss and the needs of the Homes – for that was in September, and our financial year closed in October. With all our money locked up, to clear the year without debt would be difficult, but then the promise of God came : 'Although the fig tree shall not blossom, neither shall fruit be in the vines, the labour of the olive shall fail, and the fields shall yield no

meat; the flock shall be cut off from the fold, and there shall be
no herd in the stalls; yet I will rejoice in the Lord; I will joy
in the God of my salvation.'

There and then I prayed that God would help me through,
and that during the course of the following year, which I saw
would be one of financial distress all over Scotland, He would
double the gifts to us. The result was that we were able to clear
our financial accounts with ease at the end of October, and in the
year following, when every church in Scotland, and every
philanthropic work had less money than they needed, the Orphan
Homes had double what it required. In that God honoured my
trust.

Our first church at Bridge of Weir only held four hundred,
and by-and-by it was too small for us. I prayed that the Lord
would give us a new church to hold one thousand people, and to
cost something like £5,000. We felt that we would get that money,
and that we would get it in one sum because we had asked God
to lay it on the heart of somebody to build the church. After a
year of waiting and praying, a friend came to me in the street
one day, and said, 'I'm going to build you that church you want.
Do you know what it will cost?' 'Yes,' I replied, '£5,000.'
'Well,' said my friend, 'you shall get the money when you
want it.'

It was a new song of praise to God that day, I can tell you,
and we went on to build our church. Now, even it we find too
small, and we are praying to the Lord for £2,500 to enlarge the
building, and enable us to accommodate five hundred more
worshippers.

I thought that, having got the church, we might, as we were
building a tower to hold the tank for our water supply, also get
a clock and chimes to enliven the village. So we prayed that the
Lord would send money for that purpose. I thought that about
£500 or £600 would be sufficient. While the building was
going on, we prayed for the money, and I was certain it would
come. The architect was hurrying me and pointing out that if
the clock and bells were really to go into the tower, the work
must be done at once. I told him there was no fear that the money
would not come. If the money had not come, and the tower was
completed, the placing of the clock and bells at a later period
would have meant practically taking down and rebuilding,
because with our water tank in position, the work would have
been impossible. My architect kept bothering me, but I was sure
the money would come, and one night I went home and found a
cheque for £2,000 – £1,500 to build a house, and £500 for

the clock and bells. The clock and bells cost £800, and the lady who sent the money paid the additional £300.

A village like our Homes, with 1,200 of a population, needed a good water supply for sanitary purposes. For a very long time we depended on a well, and stored the water in tanks, but frequently the supply fell short, and we felt that if we could get the proprietors in the upper district – none of the surrounding proprietors, by the way, had ever taken much interest in the work of the Homes – to give us the privilege of bringing water into the grounds, we should be able to do much to improve that state of matters. Sir Michael Shaw Stewart gave us the right to use our own burn higher up for the purpose, and gave us a piece of ground at a nominal rent of 12/- a year, for a reservoir and filter, but the money to carry out the work was not in hand, and we prayed to the Lord to send us from £1,200 to £1,400, which we anticipated would be the cost of the undertaking.

Some time later a lady called at James Morrison Street (Glasgow) and left word that an old woman who lived in Main Street, Gorbals, wished to see me. On the following day I called at the address given, and found the person who had sent for me. She was an old woman living in a single apartment, and she was very ill and weak. 'Are you Mr. Quarrier?' she asked. I said I was. 'Ye were once puir yersel',' she went on; 'I was once a puir girl with naebody to care for me, and was in service when I was eleven years old. I have been thankful for a' the kindness that has been shown to me in my life.'

She went to a chest of drawers in the corner of the apartment, and after a little came and gave me two deposit receipts on the Savings Bank, each for £200, and on neither of which any interest had been drawn for twenty years. When I cashed them I received £627.

I said 'Janet' – Janet Stewart was her name – 'are you not giving me too much?' 'Na, na, I've plenty mair, an' ye'll get it a' when I dee.'

We did the best we could for Janet, but she did not live much longer. Within a week I received a telegram that Janet was dead, and she had died, I was told singing 'Just as I am, without one plea.'

In her will she left several sums to neighbours who had been kind to her in life, and to our Homes was bequeathed the balance. Altogether the Orphans' share was £1,400. The money defrayed the cost of our water scheme, and I always think how appropriate the gift was, for nearly all her life Janet had been a washerwoman and had earned her bread over the wash-tub.

The direct answers to prayers of which I could tell you would fill a volume, and what I have mentioned are only those fixed in my memory. I have always asked God for a definite gift for a definite purpose, and God has always given it to me. The value of the buildings at Bridge of Weir is £200,000, and since we started, the cost of their 'upkeep' has been £150,000. And we are still building as busily as in the beginning.

'We are still building as busily as in the beginning', so said William Quarrier in 1897. Six more years of such building were to be his then, on 16th October 1903 the great heart was stilled. After a short period of weakness, followed by a shock and several days of unconsciousness, he died at 'Homelea', surrounded by his family. He was seventy-four years of age, and had worked hard all his days, making boots, saving souls, loving children and serving his God. When he was buried the Glasgow City Flag was lowered to half-mast at the City Chambers and a vast gathering stood by his graveside. His body rests in the fair lands of Nittingshill, alongside many of the orphans whom he had succoured. Nearby the clock in the church tower measures the passing of the hours but no one can measure what this man accomplished. His death aroused national regret and the newspaper which had published his first letter in 1864 now paid this tribute :

Mr. Quarrier was a master of detail as well as of administration. He had the quality of splendid audacity in conception, and his great faith in money coming in as it was needed carried him through. He was, it need hardly be said, a very devout man. In early life he saw and heard much that impelled him to a deeply religious life from which he never swerved. Personally he was a trifle reserved in manner, but those who knew him well admired the firm courtesy and kindness which underlay his seeming reticence. The orphan children of Scotland he took to his big heart. He founded for them homes, not charitable institutions. No charity stamp is to be seen. There is none on the buildings, or on the arrangements, or on the children. Nor is there meanness visible anywhere. The schoolrooms are as beautiful, as well appointed, and as tidy as any in the Kingdom. In the death of William Quarrier, Glasgow and the West of

Scotland mourn the loss of a powerful, and in many respects, an unique personality.

Scotland, and her folk, joined Glasgow in sorrow, but also in thanksgiving, for a life so timeously given to the land, and for faith so adventurous and true.

William Quarrier ended the 1902 'Narrative', the last he was to write, with this poem of Helen Hunt Jackson. The last verse was almost prophetic :

> 'If I can live
> To make some pale face brighten, and to give
> A second lustre to some tear-dimmed eye,
> Or e'en impart
> One throb of comfort to an aching heart,
> Or cheer some way-worn soul in passing by,
>
> 'If I can lend
> A strong hand to the fallen or defend
> The right against a single envious strain,
> My life, though bare
> Perhaps of much that seemeth dear and fair
> To us on earth, will not have been in vain.
>
> 'The purest joy
> Most dear to heaven, far from earth's alloy,
> Is bidding clouds give way to sun and shine,
> And 'twill be well
> If, on that day of days, the angels tell
> Of me, "She did her best for one of Thine".'

'LET US NOW PRAISE FAMOUS MEN AND OUR FATHERS THAT BEGAT US'.

Ecclesiasticus 44 Verse 1

CHAPTER 7

And when he died? ...

WHEN the leader of any great enterprise dies the question
is asked with urgency 'What will now happen to the work?'
Before Quarrier's death those who worked with him, and
the many who supported his children's village, must sometimes have been apprehensive when they thought of the days
to come when, inevitably, the master planner was no more
beside them to initiate and guide. In almost every sense the
achievement had been a personal one and each department
bore the imprint of William Quarrier's thinking. On the other
hand he had been brought to his task by the God he served
and when, on occasion, questions as to the future were
raised, he was content to say that the same God could be
trusted to take care of the children and their cottage homes.

In the event the work went ahead, but not without a
slowing-down in its pioneering quality. Construction went
on, maintenance did not fail, and the needs of children continued to be met. At the same time the records show that no
one came on the scene during this period with the quite
amazing spirit of adventurous effort that characterised the
founder. Perhaps this was a good thing. It made consolidation
of the work possible and time was given for an administrative
grouping to develop.

Immediately on Quarrier's death the Trustees issued this
statement:

At the date of Mr. Quarrier's death the Trustees under the deed
of constitution were Sir Thomas Glen Coats, Bart.; Sir Charles
Cameron, Bart.; Mr. Robert Binnie, Ashford, Gourock; Mr.
J. H. N. Graham, Larbert House; Mr. A. Cameron Corbett,
M.P., Thornliebank House; Mr. Alexander Forrester Paton,

Alloa; Mr. W. A. Campbell, of Messrs. J. & W. Campbell, Glasgow; and Mr. R. A. Bryden, Architect, Glasgow.

These Trustees all continue to act, and have arranged to assume as additional Trustees Sir Samuel Chisholm, Bart.; Councillor J. P. Maclay, Mr. David J. Findlay (Mr. Quarrier's son-in-law), and Mrs. Quarrier. Councillor J. P. Maclay has agreed to accept the position of honorary treasurer.

In accordance with the desire of the late Mr. Quarrier, and with the cordial approval of the Trustees, the management of the Homes will be carried on by Mrs. Quarrier and family, on the same principle as in the past, and the Trustees have appointed Mr. Bryden, Mr. Maclay, and Mr. Findlay as an advisory council, who will regularly report to them.

The Trustees do not propose to make any special appeal for subscriptions, as they consider that the system adopted by Mr. Quarrier of trusting to Divine Providence, to provide for the maintenance of the Orphan Homes should be adhered to.

On 22nd June 1904 Mrs. Isabella Quarrier died and was buried beside her husband. She had been a true and able partner and it seems fitting that she was left without him for only eight months. All accounts speak of her gentleness and serenity. Quarrier owed much to her. Her quieter nature balanced his ruggedness, and her support of all his efforts never wavered. She had been given a good education in childhood. Over the years she wrote thousands of letters for William and the Homes. With her own hands she cut out, fashioned, and made hundreds of garments for the orphan children. Her generosity was proverbial and her hospitality renowned. Without her the Orphan Homes could never have been. With her success was assured. Her own vital Christian trust matched that of her husband.

The management of the Homes now rested with Mr. and Mrs. Quarrier's two daughters; Mary, who did not marry, and Mrs. Agnes Quarrier Burges. The third sister, Isabella was married to the well-known Pastor David J. Findlay, founder of the Glasgow Tabernacle. In 1906 the Advisory Council became an Executive Committee. On 14th April of that year, Mr. R. A. Bryden, who had been Architect of the Homes from the beginning and who gave all his splendid

F

services freely, died. In the same year a new Fund appears, 'The Home and Foreign Mission Fund'. This shows at an early stage the increasing influence of Pastor Findlay who, from his Glasgow Tabernacle, was enthusiastically supporting foreign missions. In 1906 this Fund showed a disbursement of £1,005 5s. 0d. By 1919 twenty-seven overseas preachers were assisted financially, and six were wholly supported by the Fund. From 1910 all church door collections at the village Church have been set aside for this purpose. The children are thus encouraged to take an interest in other lands and peoples, as well as to give from their own pocket-money for the furtherance of the faith that brought such help to them.

During the period now under review two great Wars darkened the world. When the First World War began in 1914 there were 1,330 children in the village, 133 patients in the Sanatoria and 85 patients at the Colony. So far as can be ascertained one hundred old boys were on War service during the first year of the conflict. The 'Narrative' for 1915 gives the first pictures of lads in uniform and the 1916 'Narrative' hints at some of the problems that had to be faced :

The most outstanding feature of the internal history of the Homes during they year has been the number of soldiers' children we have been privileged to welcome. Of these, 407 have been with us for longer or shorter periods, and 59 have been returned to their friends. Our Government, which in these days pours out money so lavishly on almost everything that has to do with the War, shows the keenest economy in providing for the children of her soldiers, so that although at Bridge of Weir we have learned from long experience to purchase in the best markets at the lowest cash prices, and to make one pound sterling go considerably further than any ordinary housewife could do, yet we find it quite impossible to feed and clothe these children within the Government's limit of supply, and have to provide from our own funds the large unsupplied margin. We look on it, however, as a great privilege to be able to help the country as well as the individual family in this way, and doubtless many of these little ones who have found a temporary shelter in God's village will carry into their future lives character-building memories of their residence here.

By the end of 1917 some six hundred and seventy old boys are known to have served their country in war and when the dark years ended with the Armistice of 11th November 1918 there were 1,550 children in the Homes, 140 patients in the Sanatoria and 101 epileptic sufferers at the Colony.

Despite the agony of war and the tremendous pressures brought to bear on every family in the land the children's needs were not overlooked. In 1918 alone some £43,668 12s. 1d. had come in from donations, payments for special children and legacies. Other large sums had been forthcoming for the Sanatoria and the Colony.

In the inter-war period a minimum of one thousand children were resident in the Homes at any given time. Social conditions were changing rapidly and the need to be met was different from what it had been in the beginning. The number of orphans decreased but the number of children in need of care because of poverty and broken family situations increased, especially during the dreary years of world depression which Britain did not escape.

In 1925 the number of Trustees had dwindled because of death and those who remained took thought for the future. In order to simplify the titles held for various properties and to improve the administration of the Homes it was decided to incorporate the whole enterprise under the Companies Acts as a non-profit earning, limited company, to be known as 'The Orphan Homes of Scotland', the Board of Trade having given a licence dispensing with the use of the word 'limited'. The Certificate of Incorporation was given at Edinburgh on 30th October 1926 and makes clear, in the widest possible way, the objects for which the incorporation was established. Paragraph 3, section 4 details part of the aim thus :

> To carry on primarily among destitute or needy children, but also among adults, in need of care or treatment, Protestant Evangelical Christian, and also educational, temperance, benevolent, medical (including medical research) work, and, for these purposes, to establish and carry on homes, schools, farms,

colonies, workshops, hostels, holiday homes, retreats, sanatoria, hospitals, clinics, laboratories, or other organisations or institutions in connection therewith, at such places in the United Kingdom and abroad, as the Incorporation may determine.

and section 9 continues :

To assist in the maintenance, education, upbringing, occupational training, and the starting in life, of children or young people, even although not inmates of the homes or other premises, who may need any such assistance, and that by way of money grants or loans or otherwise as the Council may see fit.

Things have indeed moved a long way since the Jamaica Street encounter between the shoemaker and the ragged match-seller!

An interesting event took place in 1929. The Greenock tenement building in which Quarrier had been born was to be demolished. The low archway of its entrance was preserved and, at the expense of Quarrier's children in Canada, it was rebuilt at the entrance to the children's Homes as a War Memorial. Its purpose is, of course, to remind all who pass by of the young men, succoured by Quarrier and his helpers, who gave their lives to defend what Britain holds dear. It says more. It bears witness to the many throughout the land, under-privileged, often unwanted, disregarded in normal times, and not much helped by the state in pre-War years who, contrary to what might have been expected, rallied to the state's defence in the hour of peril and proved their manhood and valour on many a stricken field, right to the death. In their service they honoured a land which had not honoured them until their moment of supreme sacrifice brought forth praise.

In February 1931 Miss Mary Quarrier died and, three years later, her sister Mrs. Agnes Quarrier Burges was buried alongside her. This left an Executive Committee of only two, Pastor D. J. Findlay and Lord Maclay (Mr. Maclay had been created a Baronet in 1914 and a Peer in 1922). The Council added Mr. Hugh Brown, C.A., to the

Committee but his death in 1936 again caused a vacancy. This time the Council's choice was Dr. James Kelly who had served with them for some time. Dr. Kelly was General Secretary of the World's Sunday School Association. During his time on the Council he had shown much interest in the work at Bridge of Weir and his knowledge of the world's youth, gathered together in many countries, enabled him to shoulder his new responsibilities without great difficulty. When Lord Maclay, on account of his advanced age, retired as Chairman of the Council in 1937, Dr. Kelly succeeded him. The following year Pastor Findlay died, and this added to Dr. Kelly's work at the Homes since he now took charge of the children's Church. He preached often himself but, perhaps one of the greatest services he rendered the children and the community, was to bring to the pulpit a number of eminent Christians from many lands, including the Japanese Kagawa and the German Neimoller. In addition, a whole series of Moderators and other British church leaders were glad to lead the children and staff in worship and, in turn, gladdened many hearts by their presence.

The men who were spared to come back from the First World War in 1918 believed they had fought and won a 'war to end wars'. Alas! in 1939 their sons had to take the sad and dreadful road that again led to battle. The Armistice of 1918 turned out to be just that, and before twenty-one years had passed the same enemy had to be faced once more. This time, although the fight was carried on in far-flung fields and on all the world's oceans, the air also saw deadly duels, some of them fought out in the skies above the Homes, from where the attackers were keen to destroy the Clyde installations and shipping.

When the Second World War began there were 1,117 children in the Homes, 210 patients in the Sanatoria and 126 at the Colony. The records detail the air-raid and other precautions necessary but the imagination must be left to deal with the problem of feeding and clothing so many in years of rationing and restriction. Yet the work went on without hindrance, indeed an intensification was required to cope with the problem of soldiers' families in special need because of the times. The hospital wards were in great demand and the service freely and cheerfully given in all directions was gratefully acknowledged.

At the end of the War 1,211 children were in residence. The Sanatoria had 108 patients and the Colony 112. The total income for 1945 amounted to £146,003 10s. 7d. and the expenditure was £101,792 6s. 4d. War photographs are again seen in the 'Narratives' and the Roll of Honour names twenty-eight Quarrier's children. It is impossible to say how many former boys and girls served in the Forces. An interesting feature of this war period is the visits, on leave, of former Quarrier's boys serving in the Canadian Forces. Almost without fail their visits had two things in common. They saw again the Cottage which had been home to them, and they sat once more in their own seat in the children's church and prayed.

The war years saw an advance so far as the Homes were concerned. It was slow and tentative, but it was there. Until now boys and girls had been kept strictly apart and cottage families were not 'mixed'. This was hardly in keeping with developing 20th-century attitudes and, in 1945 Dr. Kelly reports :

You may remember that last year I made reference to an experiment that was being tried out of 'mixed cottages' so that younger boys and girls might share more fully in that Home life which the Orphan Homes sets before itself as its ideal. I am glad to inform you that this experiment has proved successful, and it has been possible to place brothers and sisters together in their early years, thus conserving the continuity of their own home life as far as possible. It is the hope of the Committee to develop this idea still further as staffing and building facilities become available.

On 18th May 1945 Mrs. Isabella Findlay, widow of Pastor Findlay, died, at the grand age of eighty-seven years. In a sense her passing marked the end of an era. No one bearing the name of Quarrier was now at Bridge of Weir. Mrs. Findlay's main work in life had been that of helpmeet to her husband and her centre of activity had long been the Tabernacle which he had founded in Glasgow. Nevertheless, especially after her father's death, she showed a constant interest in the Orphan Homes and, particularly in her Canadian visits, helped the work forward in many ways. Her body was laid in what had by then become the Quarrier burial-place alongside the children's church.

Old names go from the records, new ones appear, the work continues.

In 1951, at the age of 93 years, the first Lord Maclay died. He had long served the Homes with unflagging enthusiasm. From his home at nearby Duchal he had been able to see the village's growth throughout the years and to encourage those who lived and worked there. As long as he was fit he seldom missed worship, morning and evening, in the village church and when his earthly end came he was buried in the children's cemetery alongside the orphan children of early days and the Quarrier family.

During these years many additions, alterations and improvements were made to the property and these included five new Cottages and a splendid hospital so that the Orphan Homes numbered seventy-seven buildings in 1953. The whole of the Colony for Epileptics was erected after Mr. Quarrier's death and after fifty years it comprised nine buildings. Excluding the Sanatoria, Quarrier's Homes and the Colony now occupied ground which, including agricultural pasture land, extended to some six hundred acres.

A note made on 31st October 1952 gives the following enlightening figures:

Orphan Homes Income for the year then ending - - - - - -	£145,145 5s. 0d.
Colony for Epileptics for the year then ending - - - - - -	17,845 9s. 6d.
Home & Foreign Mission Fund Income -	977 16s. 7d.

Total amount of money received since
the beginning of the work in 1871 . . .
approximately   -   -   -   -   £4,894,613
Total number of children admitted since
1871   -   -   -   -   -   -   23,240
Total number of persons admitted to
Colony for Epileptics since the
opening in 1903   -   -   -   -   1,814

These figures give some indication of the magnitude of the need that aroused William Quarrier to action, the unfailing response, and the faithfulness of God.

In the summer of 1955 Dr. Kelly asked the Council of Management to consider the future leadership of the Homes. He had served for a long time and wished to be relieved of some of his duties. The Council members gave careful thought to the future and eventually formed a new type of administration. Dr. Kelly retired on 31st October 1956. At the Council's request he accepted the post of Honorary President and continued to act for a time as Senior Chaplain at the Homes' Church.

For twenty-five years Dr. Kelly had been associated with the life and work of the Orphan Homes and, in close association with the first Lord Maclay, had guided its path in peace and war. He travelled much in connection with his work for the World Sunday School Association and the tales he brought back to the children, of foreign lands and faraway folk, entranced and enlightened them. In his retirement he chose to live at nearby Kilmacolm and to maintain his lively interest in all the many activities of the Homes.

CHAPTER 8

And then what?

THERE were signs in 1939 that the United Kingdom Government was becoming increasingly concerned about the needs of deprived children and the help available for them. Such plans as were in mind were shelved when the Second World War came. However in 1944, with the successful end of the war in sight, the correspondence columns of *The Times*, and other newspapers, began to show the concern many responsible citizens felt about the plight of such boys and girls.

On 20th April 1945 the Secretary of State for Scotland set up what became known as the 'Clyde Committee', a group of fourteen able men and women, under the chairmanship of Mr. James L. Clyde, K.C., charged

> to be a Committee to inquire into existing methods of providing for children who from loss of parents or from any cause whatever are deprived of a normal home life with their own parents or relatives; and to consider what further measures should be taken to ensure that these children are brought up under conditions best calculated to compensate them for the lack of parental care.

The Committee did its work well and produced a comprehensive Report in July 1946. As a result a 'Children's Act' went on the Statute Book in 1948. When one considers the standard set at Quarrier's down the years in the light of the Clyde Report and the Children's Act it is at once obvious how wise and far-sighted the Founder and his successors had been. Much of what was commended and enjoined in the late forties had already been envisaged and put into practice at Bridge of Weir. Under the 1948 Act all Voluntary Homes were registered, regular inspections organised, and Government interest and authority made real. All of this was welcomed at the Orphan Homes of Scotland and the new national interest shown in those who had been the object of special love there for over seventy years, was appreciated.

By 1956 the effects of this new interest and legislation were evident. There was close co-operation with local authorities who had the responsibility of putting children under care. The background of the children admitted was quite different from that prevailing in earlier days. No longer was there such utter destitution in the land. Modern medicine had increased man's life expectation and fewer and fewer orphans were to be found. However an increasingly affluent society had not necessarily led to a better behaved, or a more responsible society, and as many children as ever were in need of care because the marriage of their parents had broken down. Further, short-term oversight of children increased, and provision was now made for boys and girls to be looked after whilst a parent or guardian was ill. The Clyde Committee had estimated that on 15th March 1945 some 17,607 children and young persons in Scotland were 'in care'. At the end of 1956, the year we have now reached in our story, 661 such children were resident at the Orphan Homes of Scotland.

This was the general background to social work with children when the Council of Management considered the future of the Homes following Dr. Kelly's decision to retire. It was evident to them that a new era had begun in the field of their labours. From now onwards liaison with statutory bodies, local authorities and Government Departments would be the order of the day. In a sense this came as a relief. For too long voluntary, religious, and philanthropic societies had had to shoulder the main burden. Now they were made part of a larger and more secure (in human terms) pattern of work. Further, their own long experience and magnificent efforts fitted them to play an important pioneering part in future plans. In the past the great work done at Bridge of

Weir had depended upon men and women of Christian character who, mainly from a sense of vocation, had given their lives in the service of children in need without asking for much reward. The same Christian character and sense of dedication would be needed in the years ahead, perhaps more so than ever. At the same time, the changed conditions demanded a measure of professionalism. Indeed, a new profession was in process of birth in the country; that of the social worker. To keep in front in its service, as had ever been the desire of its leaders, the Orphan Homes had to recognise this fact, and was quick to do so. It has been one of the glories of this particular community that all this change has not lessened the central Christian witness of the work. Whilst local authorities partly subsidise the children they ask to be taken into the Homes, the bulk of the money required still comes, unsolicited, from the 'Lord's stewards' as William Quarrier so aptly described them.

The problem the Council had to face in 1955/1956 was a difficult one. What form of administration would best suit the greatly altered circumstances of the work, and to whom would they entrust the leadership at such a critical, if exciting time? They were under no delusions as to the importance of the decisions they had to make. After much deliberation it was decided to create a new office, that of General Director. The holder would be responsible for the entire organisation, subject only to the Council. This gave a man great scope. It also laid great responsibilities upon his shoulders and required a person of outstanding character and ability.

The man was already on the staff. In 1946 Dr. J. Romanes Davidson had been appointed Medical Superintendent of the Homes and the Colony for Epileptics. Holding the degrees of M.B., Ch.B., and M.D. of the University of Edinburgh, Dr. Davidson had first practised at Bo'ness. He had then gone back to the mission station of his birth (his father having been doctor there) at South Travancore, one of the largest Medical Missions in India. During World War II he had served in the Indian Medical Service and had

commanded Hospitals in India and the Middle East. A cultured
man, of wide and varied experience, richly endowed with
human understanding and sympathy, Dr. Davidson had
proved his worth as the Homes' doctor for those ten years.
Moreover, his quiet but settled Christian faith commended
itself to thoughtful people. His wife, a fully qualified and
experienced nurse, shared all his interests and, with a warm
compassion, did much for the children and staff at the Homes.
It was to this man that the Council now turned and, with
unanimity, they asked him to be the first General Director
of the Orphan Homes of Scotland. Dr. Davidson accepted the
offer and assumed complete oversight, under the Council,
on 1st March, 1956. The years have proved the wisdom of
this choice.

Having appointed a General Director the members of the
Council now turned their minds towards the post of chairman.
They invited Mr. William H. Marr to undertake this
responsibility. He had only recently joined them but already
his sterling qualities and wide experience of men and the
world had greatly impressed his fellows. In addition to wise
business acumen Mr. Marr had a strongly developed sense
of social responsibility. He served as Glasgow Dean of Guild
and was noted for his interest in many philanthropic projects.
For ten years he was Chairman of the Council of Management
and saw the Orphan Homes develop its work and take its own
special place in the new role demanded of it in Scotland's
changing social scene.

The 1958 'Narrative' bears the title 'Quarrier's Homes'
for the first time. Until now the name had been 'The Orphan
Homes of Scotland' but it was felt the moment was ripe for a
change. In his annual report that year Dr. Davidson put it
thus:

For some time it has been considered that it would be fitting to
change the name to that of 'Quarrier's Homes', and in June of
this year this took place. While the name 'The Orphan Homes of
Scotland' has a very special significance and was the name given
by William Quarrier, there are very good reasons for making the

change. In it, we do honour to our very great founder and per-
petuate his name, and at the same time we make official a name
which has been applied to this village for many years. The
altered designation and the dropping out of the term 'orphan'
reflects also the change which has come about in the reasons for
children coming into our care. It is a remarkable fact that the
expectation of life in Scotland has risen by over twenty years
since Mr. Quarrier died in 1903. This means that it is now
unusual for children to lose both their parents, or for that matter
even one, before they have reached the age of leaving school,
which was a very common thing in his day. The change of name
is also of obvious benefit to our children.

Soon after this change, on 7th July, the Homes were
honoured by a visit from H.M. The Queen. This was the
first royal visit to the children's village.

After a number of presentations Her Majesty heard the
children's choir sing the Bach Chorale, 'O Light of Life'.
She then presented prizes to the Dux boy and girl, the
Junior Dux, and to two boys nominated for the Outward
Bound Moray Sea School. As Her Majesty left the Church
she signed the Visitors' Book and passed a Guard of Honour
drawn from the seven uniformed organisations. She then
called at Cottage Three and met the family of seventeen
children. After the Queen had gone all the village children
celebrated the visit with special entertainments and sports in
the playing fields. Perhaps the most enduring memory of the
visit was the singing of the children as the Queen entered
their church. Did the five hundred voices raise a Psalm of
Supplication . . . a hymn of faith, maybe. . . ? No. Quite
significantly this rousing chorus greeted the Sovereign :

'Count your blessings, name them one by one;
    Count your blessings, see what God hath done;
Count your blessings, name them one by one,
    And it will surprise you what the Lord hath done!'

In such fashion do Scottish children in care encourage their
Queen!

Four years later H.R.H. Princess Margaret visited the

village. The Central Building, Mr. Quarrier's first construction, had been completely renovated and now included a
magnificent Hall for Concerts, Drama, and social gatherings.
Here the Princess unveiled a commemorative plaque and
described the Homes as 'a charitable work launched in faith
and still continued in faith in God and faith in our fellow men'.

In 1965, when a new Superintendent came to be appointed,
the office was named 'Deputy Director and Superintendent'.
It went to one of the first holders of Edinburgh University's
Certificate of Social Studies, an indication of the increasing
professional approach to child care.

On moving to the east coast in 1966 Mr. Marr gave up
office as Chairman but continued to act as Honorary Treasurer.
In his place the Council appointed the second Lord Maclay.
From his earliest days Lord Maclay knew the Homes and
had maintained his father's great interest in them as well as
in many other philanthropic movements. A good servant
of his country he embodied all that is best in the Scottish
character. For many years he was National President of the
Boys' Brigade. In all places where he served, the world of
business, Parliament, the Church, and not least, at Quarrier's
Homes, he was a respected and much loved figure. He knew
the children well and developed an increasing interest in the
Colony for Epileptics and the patients there. With Lady
Maclay he did much for the wellbeing of the children and
staff and his death, only three years after taking up the
Chairmanship, occasioned real sorrow. In his first public
speech as Chairman he said :

> My father and family have had a long connection with Quarrier's
> Homes, right from the time of Mr. Quarrier, and I would like
> to assure you that I will try my very best to make some con-
> tribution also. . . . This audience does not need me to tell you
> that we are passing through strange and very stirring days and
> Quarrier's Homes like everywhere else, must feel the impact of
> new ideas and scientific progress. I would like you to know that
> it is the ambition of the Council and the Executive to try and
> keep fully in touch with everything in the way of progress, new
> knowledge and thought, that may help the efficient running of

these Homes. . . . I believe that our faith in God's influence and interest in this work is as strong and commanding today as it was in William Quarrier's time. We realise we have to try and interpret that faith in the midst of a restless and materialistic age, amidst difficulties for adults and for children, especially young children going out from here into this peculiar world that we find around us today.

I would like to say this, that on our 95th Thanksgiving Meeting, we give thanks for past achievements, for all that those who have gone before us have achieved and done for this place, and we now today, at this our Thinaksgiving, humbly ask God's help to enable us to carry on the work, – the Council, the Executive, staff, workers and friends, – and to carry it on in a manner pleasing to God's will.

In all Lord Maclay's work for the Homes, before and during his Chairmanship, he stood firmly for this ideal and faith.

As the nineteen-sixties came to an end, then, the Homes faced the future with a competent Director, ably supported by a resident Superintendent, Secretary, Doctor, Chaplain, Matrons, Nurses, Farmer, Tradesmen, Psychologist, Youth Leaders, After-care Officers, Training Tutor, Headmaster and Teachers, Fire Prevention Officer, Clerk of Works, Steward, and, most important of all, a splendid band of house parents and cottage aunties, all of them charged, in their several ways, with the high privilege of caring for, moulding, instructing and inspiring little children.

During this period the maintenance of buildings was given high priority. Kitchens, bathrooms, entire cottages, were inspected and, very often, completely modernised. New and up-to-date fittings were installed and life made somewhat easier for the cottage mother, aunt and cleaner. In this matter great service was rendered by the Ladies' Committee, set up in March, 1959, and presided over by Lady Maclay. The members of this Committee visit each cottage monthly and establish friendly contact with the house mother and, often, with the children. From time to time the schedule of visits is rearranged so that eventually each visitor gets to know almost the whole community. A notable event in 1960 was the provision of a television set in each home.

Great improvements have been effected at the farm and in 1967 the manager came home rejoicing from the Kilbarchan Show, carrying many awards won by his cattle beasts. The finest milk is provided daily from the Homes' farm and this doubtless contributes to the excellent health of children and adults.

One of William Quarrier's great dreams was to have a swimming pool for his children. He did not see this brought about but, at last, in March, 1966, a magnificent pool was opened by Bobby McGregor, the Scottish Olympic swimmer. In addition to opening the new pool Mr. McGregor marked the occasion by setting a new time for swimming two lengths of the baths. The pool has proved tremendously beneficial and is greatly appreciated by both children and staff. Almost every child over eight years of age can now swim and the confidence with which even the youngest manages in the water is admirable. Another boon came along in 1968 when a large and useful Recreation Centre was erected adjacent to the playing fields.

Nor was the Colony for Epileptics forgotten in all this growth. Dr. Davidson continued to take a personal, and particular, interest in this part of the work. He is a recognised European authority on epilepsy and the Colony he has developed at Bridge of Weir is a model of its type, and remains the sole hospital in Scotland entirely set apart for the treatment of this illness. In 1965 a school was built for epileptic children. The existing Colony buildings have been modernised and maintained, workshops have been established, and new methods of industrial employment undertaken. Already in 1957 Dr. Davidson reported :

A new eight-channel Electro-encephalograph was installed in April of this year to replace the four-channel instrument that has been doing excellent service for the past eight-and-a-half years. The new and larger machine is even more helpful in localising abnormal electrical areas of the brain and aiding in the diagnosis of epilepsy. An increasing number of children have been referred for examination and opinion by the physicians of the Royal Hospital for Sick Children, Glasgow, and the Counties of Renfrew, and Ayr. This has probably resulted in less children requiring to be admitted for treatment.

The growing recognition of the work done at the Colony was emphasised when, at a Conference in Paris during 1967 under the auspices of The International Bureau for Epilepsy, a report was given and received with appreciation, on the industrial therapy work done at Bridge of Weir. Dr. Davidson plays a full part in international concern for the relief and healing of epileptic patients and in such circles the Quarrier Colony is highly regarded. It remains a private hospital and is not under the management of the Department of Health.

The most recent addition, and the eleventh building at the Colony, is Hunter house. Named in honour of Mrs. Quarrier this is a modern purpose-built unit which provides extremely comfortable accommodation for twenty-four patients. The 'Narrative' for 1969 records :

> The aim is to use the additional accommodation for epileptic patients who do not require long-term care but who, during a comparatively short stay can be assessed, have their treatment stabilised and thereafter be able to return to suitable work in the general community.

So, here too, in this centre, unique in Scotland, the vision granted William Quarrier in his latter years has not dimmed. Still pioneering, still serving, still loving, those who man this Colony give thanks, not only for the vision given so long ago, but, just as heartily, for the blessing which has never been absent, and which is there to lift up the hearts of patients and staff today.

On 7th November 1969, just as the decade came to its close, Lord Maclay died. At a Memorial Service in the Homes Church Dr. Davidson said :

> Today, as we gather here, out thoughts are on a man to whom this village, and particularly this Church, meant a very great deal. Joseph Paton, Baron Maclay, whose passing we mourn,

G

was brought here by his parents to Sunday services in his early childhood and probably later as a somewhat reluctant schoolboy home on holiday from Fettes College. The faith that he learnt and the everlasting truths of the Christian Gospel that he heard remained sincerely and honestly with him all his days.

In his place the Council appointed his younger brother the Rt. Hon. Viscount Muirshiel, C.H., C.M.G. In accepting this office the new Chairman continues the long and intimate connection of the Maclay family with the village. On 13th September 1958, as the Rt. Hon. John S. Maclay, Secretary of State for Scotland, he had visited the Homes and unveiled a plaque which had been placed on the wall of the Founder's home. On that occasion he revealed his knowledge of the Homes and the work carried on there and related it to the national pattern of child-care. He said :

. . . From the personal point of view, speaking from this platform I must confess is thoroughly alarming. It could really hardly be otherwise. It must be about fifty years ago that I first came into this Church. I suspect that I was carried in, faintly protesting, and the whole building is filled with very vivid memories for me. I was too young, of course, to know Mr. and Mrs. Quarrier, but Miss Quarrier, Mrs. Burges, Pastor Findlay, no one, whether grown up or a child as I was when I first met them, could possibly forget or fail to have been permanently influenced by the love and understanding which their whole lives and their lives' work represented.

These fifty years have seen vast changes in our ideas of social responsibility; the part which individuals can play, the part which we now know the State must play; but it is undoubtedly true that it is out of the acute sense of personal responsibility felt by men like William Quarrier that the best of our modern ideas have sprung. . . .

Mr. Quarrier, for example, was a pioneer and he left no body of written doctrine behind. He expected that the work he founded would survive so long as there were children in need of a good home. In the course of the years he made all sorts of adjustments to make certain that they got the best kind of surroundings possible, and because of this very freedom and flexibility, Quarrier's Homes have been able to keep abreast of changing experience so that today this Village is even more famous than it was when Mr. Quarrier died years ago. It would be strange and indeed, tragic, if nothing had been learned about the care and upbringing of the young in the eighty-one years since the foundation stone was laid here at Bridge of Weir. Throughout the world, thank goodness, Quarrier has been followed by others, a great many of them inspired by his experience. Statutory as well as voluntary organisations now abound to look after and help the young, and men and women are still found in numbers who are prepared to place their entire experience in the service of children. If Mr. Quarrier could stand with us today, I am certain he would have rejoiced at this extension of a work of which he was a very great pioneer. . . .

It would be a matter for despair if it were ever to be thought that our country could get on without men such as Mr. Quarrier was. However much an all-powerful and beneficent State may try to do for people and above all for the young, it can never take the place of men of vision and compassion.

Another Secretary of State for Scotland was to pay his tribute to William Quarrier eleven years later. Speaking at the annual Thanksgiving gathering on 27th September 1969, the Rt. Hon. William Ross said :

William Quarrier was decades before his time. He was a tremendous pioneer in the work of Sanatoria in the early years of the Century. In 1903 after he died the Epilepsy Colony was actually opened.

You know, it was not until 1948, and he started his real work in 1864 for children, that Parliament passed for Scotland a Bill which said that every Local Authority should have a Children's Committee – that is how far ahead of his time he was. Children are still the most vulnerable section of our community, subject to all the emergencies of family life and all the frailties and all the things that happen to them often through no fault of their own. So as we move on I am perfectly sure that what was started and what was continued by William Quarrier will still provide and find a solution to the newer problems of today. . . .

I think that our presence here is not just a tribute to a man but a tribute to that man's abiding faith, and that faith which was justified by everything that happened. . . . As human beings, as communities, we have been away way behind the William Quarriers of this world. We are just catching up. . . . I am perfectly certain that generations in Scotland will still remember with thanksgiving and affection that great Christian, William Quarrier, who believed not just in Christianity, but in the practical application of the lessons of the Gospel.

So, as the Centenary of his great work drew near, William Quarrier was lauded by the foremost men in the nation, named with thanksgiving by the grandchildren of those he had first helped, and praised when, in the Sanctuary he built, little children, still being cared for, thanked God for good and famous men.

CHAPTER 9

What of Today and Tomorrow?

On 27th September 1969 Dr. Davidson reported to the 98th Annual General Meeting of the Homes:

> ... At present we have five hundred children resident either here at Bridge of Weir, or at 'Overbridge' in Glasgow, or 'Merton' at Largs. There are also thirty-five boarded out in private homes throughout Scotland. The number in our care has remained stationary for the last ten years and this in spite of a very large admission and discharge rate. Requests for admisson never get less. It would appear that we may need to increase our accommodation. In the whole field of Child Care the number looked after does not diminish – a tragic situation in our present civilisation.
>
> The new Social Work Act is now with us and I can assure everyone we will continue to co-operate fully with the Social Work Departments and their Central Organisations as we have done in the past with the many Children's Departments. We know we can rely in the future on the Government advisers for their help and good advice as we have had up-to-date.
>
> To care for so many costs a lot of money but the '20th Century Miracle' still continues and as we come to the end of another financial year next Tuesday I know we will have balanced our very large budget. In these days of rising costs it is truly a modern miracle and we thank God with all humility and sincerity. There are so many who give generously to make this possible.

In addition to the five hundred children being cared for there were at that date one hundred and fifty-two resident patients at the Colony.

Income that year from Legacies, Bequests, Donations and Maintenance amounted to £366,603 15s. 4d. and it was costing approximately £1,000 a day to maintain the whole establishment. Quite a business – with Faith in God as its principal asset!

It is often asked why so many children require to be put into care today. Quarrier's Homes analysed the reasons behind the admissions for the year ending 30th September 1969 as follows:

No parent or guardian	1
Abandoned or lost	2
Parents in desertion	61
Infirmity of parent or guardian confinement-	10
Mental illness	17
Short-term physical illness	24
Other physical illness	12
Eviction	15
Parent or guardian in prison	13
Child illegitimate and mother unable to provide	17
Other reasons	70
Under Fit Person Order-	28
	270

When children arrive they find themselves at home in a selected Cottage family. Normally each cottage has fourteen children making up the circle. They are cared for by a house father and mother in most cases, although, now and again, one finds a Cottage Mother managing quite adequately along with the assistants provided. The house Fathers engage in other duties in the Homes for part of the day. The family schedule is not greatly different from that elsewhere. There is the morning bell, breakfast, getting ready for school, with all the accompanying tantrums. During lessons the Cottage Mother and Aunt, helped by the cleaner, are putting the house in order and preparing the main mid-day meal. At noon the hungry children hurry home and quickly devour well cooked, substantial food. Then off to school again until four o'clock. Tea follows, then homework, and in summer time plenty of fun and games in the park, the playing fields, the tennis courts, or on the cottage lawns.

In wet summer weather, and in the winter, the Youth Leaders continue their good work inside the vast Recreation Centre. Then there are extra private lessons in music, voice production, dancing and so on, for all who wish. In addition there are weekly meetings of the Boys' Brigade, the Junior Brigade, the Boy Scouts and Cubs, the Girl Guides and Girls' Brigade, and the Army Cadets, when members participate in all that is common to the organisation, fraternise with outside companies and troops, and plan for week-end and summer camps. The Army Cadets have been particularly keen in working for the Duke of Edinburgh's Awards and have gained, for a beginning, four Bronze Medals, whose holders now press towards higher prizes. A mixed Youth Club meets each evening and the activities are both educational and recreational. There is, in fact, nothing lacking here for body, mind and spirit, and to meet the children and talk to them, speedily dispels any misconception the visitor may bring about 'institutionalism' or 'deprivation'.

But soon, too soon always, night comes and it is time for bed. In the baby and toddler Homes the very little ones are already asleep. In the children's cottages prayers of thanksgiving are said, tired little bodies and gradually-quietening minds go to rest and, after a while (which may seem an eternity to a house-parent!) all is silent.

As far as possible the house-parent irons out the child's individual problems. Where this is not possible he has beside him, at a moment's call, the teacher, doctor, minister, social worker, matron, psychologist, superintendent, General Director, all there at the willing service of each child. What a wealth of experience and compassionate skill this place holds! The word 'holds' is wrong. Such help is not held. It is freely given, and very frequently used well beyond the confines of the Children's Village.

The week-ends are, of course, different. Very often parents take their children home for the Saturday, or for the week-end. The objective is to heal the family, where there has been a marriage breakdown, and in all circumstances to make possible the eventual reunion of child with parent or parents. Again, many of the children have foster friends who take them for trips on a Saturday afternoon. When they are not away themselves they welcome freely, and with a child's curiosity, the house parents' relatives and friends who come to call.

Sunday is the day of worship. As the church bell rings the cottage family makes its way to its own pew. Each boy is smartly dressed, some colourful in the kilt. Each girl is a picture in modern and bright dress. In the summer a perfect rash of straw bonnets may be seen, although the wearing of a hat is certainly not required.

Often the children participate in the Service and they take part very naturally and well. Like all well-brought-up Scots, they are great 'sermon-tasters', and pity the poor minister who comes to their church unprepared, or any preacher who begins to 'talk down' to his hearers!

At the evening service mission choruses are sung with great gusto and are repeated in many a cottage later on. In this church there is little formality, great participation, joyful worship, and an abiding sense of the real presence of God in the remembrance of bread that has come day by day for a hundred years. As each Sunday in church comes to an end, little heads are bowed, little hands are clasped, and children's voices sing their special vesper. Scarcely anywhere else in the world can the hymn have such meaning as here:

'Jesus, tender Shepherd, hear me;
    Bless Thy little lamb tonight;
Through the darkness be Thou near me;
    Watch my sleep till morning light.

'All this day Thy hand has led me,
    And I thank Thee for Thy care;
Thou hast clothed me, warmed and fed me:
    Listen to my evening prayer.

'Let my sins be all forgiven;
    Bless the friends I love so well;
Take me, when I die, to heaven,
    Happy there with Thee to dwell.'

We live in an age of specialisation and intensive training in a chosen field. Quarrier's Homes has recognised this and, in recent years, emphasis has been laid upon the necessity and benefits of training. Social Workers on the staff are seconded to full-time courses of one or two years' duration when places can be found at the various Universities and Colleges. They then return to their work with increased knowledge and ability and, often, with a new enthusiasm. For the house parents actually on the spot and doing the job the Homes organise their own 'In Service' Courses. At the first of such Courses during 1969/70 fourteen members of Quarrier's own staff and five residential workers from other Homes attended and gained the appropriate Certificate.

In 1965, out of 54 house-parents, only eight had been trained. By 1970 there were 48 house-parents and half of them had attended Courses. Of the remaining twenty-four, ten were not in need of training since each held the Certificate of Recognition, awarded after ten years in the work. The fourteen left without specialist training will attend courses during the period 1970/72.

The Homes also assists in the training of others. On 22nd May 1970 it was reported to the Executive Committee :

During the past academic year, from September onwards, we have had with us for training periods, the following students :

  3 from residential child care courses at Glasgow and Aberdeen;
  1 from Dundee University;
14 graduates from Glasgow University;
  6 from Callendar Park College, Falkirk;
14 from Barmulloch College, Glasgow;
15 social workers from Lanarkshire and Paisley Social Work Departments.

Surely this would have gladdened William Quarrier's heart!

The children's education, too, is carefully attended to. In addition to Carsemeadow School for epileptic children, there is the William Quarrier School within the grounds, built by Quarrier, and for long now administered by Renfrew County Council. In Quarrier's day a good education was something of a luxury for many, although in the world of education Scotland was well advanced. The country had three Universities before the Reformation of 1560, the oldest at St. Andrews being inaugurated in 1410, and ranking third oldest in the United Kingdom, coming after Oxford and Cambridge. John Knox had as his ideal at the Reformation, a Kirk, a Minister, a School, and a Schoolmaster in every Parish in the land. He worked hard to provide this. At the time of Robert Burns (1759–96) it was possible for his father, not a wealthy man, to pay the penny a week, or so, all that was required, to give Robert and his brothers a good grounding in knowledge. His training was thoroughly literary as 'he was exercised in turning verse into prose, selecting synonyms, and so forth'. In the 19th century in Scotland many a 'lad o' pairts' was singled out by the village, or parish dominie, encouraged, enlightened, and aided right on to University and Degree standard. The world is richer for them. Yet the children Quarrier succoured had not much chance of such opportunities and he was determined to give them the rudiments of education. He provided school and teachers and encouraged the children in their lessons. It is to his credit, and their own, that many of them succeeded in life well beyond the long dreams of youth. The William Quarrier School is an abiding witness to his interest in the pursuit of knowledge and his faith in the pupils and teachers who would work there.

It has to be admitted that the school has special problems. Children coming into care often register low intelligence quotients. This does not necessarily mean that they are mentally backward. More often it is a result of the unfortunate circumstances which have brought them to the Homes. Again, there is a continual coming and going of pupils, as children are admitted and then discharged. Further it is difficult to get, and hold on to, staff, and there are numerous changes in the ranks of the teachers.

However, over the years quite a number of pupils have gone on to Secondary Schools and University from the Village School and many Quarrier's boys and girls are to be found in the ranks of the professions, at home and abroad. Some work in the Foreign Mission field; some are in industry and commerce; some are doctors and ministers. All remember with affection the School at Quarrier's and those who taught them there.

A Nursery School has long been in existence. It is open during the mornings. In the afternoons special care and individual attention are given to the small group of pre-school children who have particular problems or difficulties.

Quarrier's Homes is not an Adoption Society but it has on occasion, boarded out children with approved foster parents. This was, until recently, considered good policy at the national level. There are signs today that the whole question of fostering requires more careful thought. Theoretically the scheme is good but, in practice, there are many problems, too many perhaps for universal approval to be given. No doubt 'fostering' is right, – for the right child and the right foster parents! But how difficult it is to bring the two together! If the child to be fostered is beyond the baby age the tendency is for him to grow up with a sense of indebtedness to his foster parents. Perhaps this sense ought to be present, but a young adolescent may feel that this is a debt he himself did not incur, and resentment can result. On the side of the foster parents the temptation towards possessiveness is very real and it requires balanced character to establish and maintain a good relationship in such a situation. On the other hand, sometimes the results are excellent. In one such happy case, where two children are fostered with parents who have one child of their own there exists a real family unit which can bring hurt to no one. This family lives in 'the house of many medals' since the mother/foster mother encourages her own son and her foster son to excel in Highland dancing and the walls are covered with medals and trophies won at many a Highland Gathering.

When June ends and School closes for the summer there is a great exodus. Each cottage family goes off for a fortnight's holiday to the place of its own choice. Not all go at once, and there is always plenty of life at Bridge of Weir. Aberdeen, Broughty Ferry, Helensburgh, Fife, the Homes' own house at Girvan, are all prime favourites. Here, in complete relaxation, the children and their house-parents, 'let off steam', and build up strength of body and mind for the next winter. Such holidays are eagerly anticipated and some of the little ones begin to pack for their summer break on Hogmanay!

Holidays are not confined to the summer months, however. In recent years, thanks to the vision and generosity of Mr. Niall D. Hodge, a whole complex of holiday cottages has been made available to Quarrier's Homes at Turnberry estate all the year round. In addition a splendid swimming pool has been opened there and 'Turnberry' has become a central talking-point and a well-loved place for the children. Plans are afoot to develop this complex and to bring it well into various training schemes envisaged for winter, as well as summer, months.

In his 1969 Report Dr. Davidson spoke of the new Social Work (Scotland) Act. This legislation has been given a warm welcome in Scotland and is both constructive and bold. It 'tidies up' areas of social responsibility and administration, and further advances the concern of all for the plight of the needy. In its working, voluntary bodies, like Quarrier's Homes, will have an important part to play. Because of their traditional freedom they are more able to experiment, and long experience gives them wisdom as they do so. This is the role, indeed, to which they are now encouraged. Experiment has always been the order of the day at Bridge of Weir and it is a field gladly occupied. Already the leadership has concerned itself with the adolescent having his first minor confrontation with authority. The violence and gang warfare all too common in some of our cities might be prevented if the up-and-coming gangster is befriended and guided at an early

stage. To prevent is always better than to cure and, with this
in mind, small groups of such lads have been brought
together. During 1969 from a housing scheme in one of
Scotland's great cities, twelve boys were brought to the
Homes for a two-week 'Adventure Course'. The boys were
from families 'at risk' and known to the local Social Workers.

The results were so good that in 1970, at Turnberry, a
three-week 'Adventure Course' was organised for another
twelve boys between the ages of twelve and fourteen years.
Again good resulted although all admit the importance of
the follow-up in such work. Not the least impressive thing
to note about this experimental child-care is the growing
association of those who serve in voluntary organisations
and those who find their work with the statutory authorities.
This co-operation augurs well for the child, the leaders and
the nation. The aim of these ·Courses is put thus by the
Superintendent :

> The purpose of this course is to take a boy who appears to be
> heading for delinquency by his anti-social behaviour and to :
>
> (a) Give him the opportunity to learn, and become interested
> in, types of activities that are already available, but not
> used by such boys, in their own community. Such activities
> are to be seen as an alternative to vandalism or even isolation.
>
> (b) Help him to find through team living and team participation,
> his own potential, to function as a member of a team, and,
> by increasing his personal achievement, to offer more to the
> team. The delinquent is so often a 'loner' in society that if
> he can become a social being his delinquency may be arrested.
>
> (c) Develop a better and deeper understanding between the
> policeman, or social worker, and the particular boy in his
> care to act as a foundation of relationships for the future.

As time goes on the present-day leaders at Quarrier's
Homes will most certainly follow the Founder in searching
out areas of greatest need and then engage to the full in
experimental care planned to meet that need.

It might be thought that such a village as Quarrier's would
tend to be isolated and self-contained. No greater error could
be made. Already in William Quarrier's day there were many

contacts with Canada. Others, in India and New Zealand, came to discuss with Quarrier and his successors, the establishment and maintenance of similar Homes in their countries.

World-wide mission interests, dating from Pastor Findlay's time, and the visits on holiday, of old boys and girls from all over the globe, keep the windows of the imagination wide open. In more recent days Quarrier's children have taken part in popular school cruises to countries of Europe and North Africa. Others have visited the Continent of Europe independently. There have been exchanges between Danish and Quarrier's boys and girls, and a regular supply of Danish house 'aunties' keeps their northern language ringing in the young folks' ears. Dutch assistants also come to work at the Homes and quite a few American students spend part of their social training periods at Quarrier's. The average child leaving the Homes at the age of fifteen would know as much, if not more, about the world and its peoples as any child of that age anywhere.

The law requires that children under care must not remain at the Homes beyond school leaving age unless they are undertaking further education.

This does not mean that they are then forgotten. Children leaving Bridge of Weir fall into two categories. There are those who have been placed in the Homes voluntarily and there are others placed in care by Local Authorities. In the case of the 'voluntary children' it is required that the Homes should care for each until he reaches the age of eighteen years, and this requirement is willingly undertaken. Indeed, in most cases, the interest and concern continue long after the eighteenth birthday. When the young man or girl, leaves, a suitable job is found, then proper lodgings. The financial position is examined and all that is needed to give him financial independence is made available. A complete clothing outfit is provided. Monthly visits from an after-care representative of the Homes take place and the young apprentice or shop-girl is encouraged to talk freely to the visitor and to regard his former cottage at Quarrier's Homes as a haven and home. Almost all do and their frequent visits are a delight to cottage parents and to the younger children.

The same procedure is followed in the case of 'Local Authority children' when the Authority asks that this should be done, although the responsibility lies on their shoulders.

When a child takes higher education he remains in his Cottage, going from there to school, until the time comes for him to enter University. He is then helped to find good lodgings, his finances are taken care of, fees are attended to as required, constant contact is maintained, and the student knows that his Cottage door at Bridge of Weir is always open for him. The unexpected meeting with an old boy or girl in one of the wide avenues of the Homes is one of the delights of the place and cottage parents, no less than the Director himself, are interested and enthralled by the reports of progress that are given when the 'old ones' return.

We are coming near the end of our tale. What a splendid road we have travelled! We have met history, the growth of social justice and concern in our land, the names of many both prominent and humble. Our journey has taken us through a period of almost unbelievable change and has included two World Wars and an era of dark depression. The William Quarrier whose work we have looked at was born when George IV reigned and we bring the story to an end when Elizabeth is on the throne, seven reigns later. Conditions for all classes in the United Kingdom have altered. The national wealth is more evenly spread and yesterday's grandfathers would be amazed to see the houses, bathrooms, television sets, motor cars and refrigerators of their children's children. When William Quarrier was born the 'safety bicycle' was unknown. Today man may travel to, and stand upon, the moon.

Three things are unchanged :

There are still many children who need love and care.
God is still in control and He continues to provide.
He still needs men and women through whom He may work.

So we return to 27th September 1969 and the 98th Annual General Meeting. The scene is set in the children's Church.

The General Director stands in exactly the position often occupied by William Quarrier. From the centre of the great platform he looks upon some two thousand upturned faces, young and old. Around him sit eminent leaders in Church and State, members of the Council of Management and senior members of staff. The Secretary of State for Scotland is the day's principal speaker. Around the church lies the unique Children's Village, now numbering eighty-one buildings. Across the road is the Colony of Mercy. The mortal remains of William Quarrier lie under the shadow of the Church but surely his spirit is in this place.

Dr. Davidson's mind goes back to the day of small beginnings, and to the fatherless shoemaker, who, under God, made it all possible. He says :

We give thanks for the memory of our Founder whose vision, hard work and faith built these Homes. In fifteen years he built thirty cottages, the Store and Laundry, the Workshops and this Church. What a physical accomplishment! However, he valued much more the spiritual things of this life, Faith in God, Hope for needy children, and Love of all men.

At Thanksgiving we pause to say thank you to many people but let us also give thanks to God who continues to bestow His blessing on us, and we acknowledge His never-failing grace to us all, for without Him we are of little account.

Epilogue

THE tale is told.

Each book we read leaves its mark on us. Each one of us is the end result of the many and varied impressions that impinge upon our senses. Not the least important source of such impressions is the printed word. We are conscious of some such influences, others we scarcely recognise. Yet it is true that each impression counts, that each tale marks us, that each story adds to our totality as human beings.

What, then, is the message of this book? The account given of William Quarrier's life and work, and its sequel, almost inevitably leads to the asking of this question.

The answer lies in the Christian Faith, the source and centre of Mr. Quarrier's life. Christianity is, amongst other things, the faith of One whose prayer was not answered, in the sense that the Cross was not taken away; and yet was answered, in the sense that the Suffering Servant, accepting that Cross, became the world's Redeemer. The Cross was not removed, and thus the deeper prayer, that God's will for Christ be not defeated by the Cross, was answered. The deeper prayer could not have been answered had the earlier petition been granted. So the Christian faith tells of triumph through suffering, a prayer unanswered leading to a greater prayer answered. So it can be with poverty and cruel suffering. The thing unwanted, and agonisingly present, can be offered to God, with the prayer that despite this 'thorn in the flesh', indeed through this unwelcome intrusion, one may reach his true fulfilment and render his own unique service to mankind and Creator. This is part of what Christianity means by salvation.

H

Here, then, is one message this study brings to the reader. William Quarrier triumphed through suffering, – early suffering and bitter experience, – offered to God. He had been given his own unique personality and he had his own special work to do in the world. After his conversion he knew that all his past story had both meaning and power if properly harnessed. Although his childhood experiences were bitter, no bitterness was allowed to remain in his heart. Only a mighty love and care for unfortunate children reigned there. Yoked with Christ, the result was inevitable, the life of concern and faith was lived gloriously. Thousands of boys and girls in the past hundred years have been deeply in Quarrier's debt, in some cases for life itself, in every case for quality of life.

So we see that suffering and deprivation, properly handled, can lead to the fully stretched life, the true expression of the unique self, the liberation of every constructive energy a man possesses. Undoubtedly this is what Christian disciple-ship meant for William Quarrier. The result of such disciple-ship is seen, not only in the stone and mortar of an entire children's village, but, even more decisively, in the life stories of the boys and girls who found shelter, hope, and God, within its walls.

This book also belies the idea that the Christian life is, of necessity, a dull life. Quarrier's story is one of great adventure. There is no dullness around when one has to feed some twelve hundred children on faith's resources! Just as God constantly chooses ordinary men and women to do extraordinary things for Him, so He colours their days by attending to their needs in curious, apparently way-out ways. The life of complete faith is a many-splendoured thing, the only certainty being sur-prise and vividness.

The tale told further confronts the reader with the power of Christian belief. For many, belief is too academic a thing. We consent with the mind, perhaps with the heart, but are never fully committed. Such was not the case with William Quarrier. Every fibre of his being was alive with faith, and his faith was not simply academic, it was active, practical, simple, and total. He believed the Gospel, he put its precepts into practice with the trust of a little child, he took God's promises as valid. The result amazed his contemporaries and the continuing work still puts to shame the scorn of the cynic. God, for Quarrier, was an ever-present Father who could be asked to supply his children with potatoes one day, and with a splendid Church the next. Both requests were, in fact, made. Both were adequately answered!

These pages also speak to us of the primacy of compassion. Without the out-going heart, tensed by the tenacious will, all our work in the service of others is incomplete. Just as William Quarrier's faith and commitment were total, so his love was with the whole heart. No amount of training, good intentions, professionalism, will avail if this compassion is lacking. When it is present nothing is impossible. Love never fails.

What, then is here for me?
A Challenge to use my Sufferings as a road to Triumph;
A Challenge to abandon myself to the life of Christian Adventure;
A Challenge to Believe the Gospel;
A Challenge to be Unafraid of the Compassionate Heart.

And if I do not have the courage to accept this fourfold challenge? Then perhaps a little child may lead me:

> 'I helped a little child to see
> That God had made a willow tree,
> And He became more real to me.
>
> 'I tried to lead a child through play
> To grow more Christ-like every day,
> And I myself became that way.
>
> 'I joined a little child in prayer,
> And as we bowed in worship there,
> I felt anew God's loving care.
>
> 'Lord, keep us ever quick to see
> By guiding children we find Thee.'

Quarrier's Homes

1971

Dr. James Kelly, O.B.E., J.P., Honorary President

Council of Management

The Rt. Hon. Viscount Muirshiel, C.H.,
C.M.G., LL.D., Chairman

Rev. J. Barr, B.Sc., Ph.D., B.D.
Robert Brough, O.B.E.
Kenneth J. Brown, C.A.
Liston Carnie, C. Eng., F.I.C.E.,
  M.Cons.E.
Thomas R. Craig, C.B.E., T.D.,
  LL.D.
Fred. A. Donaldson
James T. Dowling, C.A.
  (Honorary Treasurer)
Rev. George B. Duncan, M.A.

Prof. J. H. Hutchison, C.B.E.,
  M.D., F.R.C.P.
Ian A. Laird
Duncan C. Leggat
Rev. William J. Morris, B.D.,
  Ph.D.
Lady Maclay
Alexander B. Murdoch
James J. Swan, J.P.
Mrs. T. P. Spens

Executive Committee

Viscount Muirshiel
Lady Maclay
Alexander B. Murdoch
James T. Dowling
Thomas R. Craig

Ian A. Laird
Robert Brough
Kenneth J. Brown
Liston Carnie
Fred A. Donaldson

General Director : J. Romanes Davidson, O.B.E., M.D.

Deputy Director/Superintendent

Joseph Mortimer

Secretary

Alex. Bonella, F.I.A.C.

Bibliography

The Life Story of Wm. Quarrier by John Urquhart (Partridge & Co., 1901)

William Quarrier by Alex. Gammie (Pickering & Inglis, 1937)

Pastor D. J. Findlay by Alex. Gammie (Pickering & Inglis, 1949)

A History of Scotland by J. D. Mackie (Penguin Books, 1964)

English Saga by Arthur Bryant (Collins, 1940)

Memoirs of the Late Dr. Barnardo by Mrs. Barnardo & J. Marchant (Hodder & Stoughton, 1907)

Barnardo of Stepney by A. E. Williams (George Allen & Unwin, Ltd., 1943)

Father of Nobody's Children by Norman Wymer (Hutchinson Authors, Ltd., 1955)

The Life of George Müller by W. H. Harding (Morgan & Scott, 1914)

Autobiography of George Müller compiled by G. Fred Bergin (J. Nisbet & Co., 1906)

The Age of Elegance by Arthur Bryant (Collins, 1950)

The Story of Burnside by R. G. Macintyre (Stag Bulletins, Parramatta, Australia)

An Introduction to the Child Care Service by John Stroud (Longmans, 1965)

Child Care Pioneers by Margaret Weddell (The Epworth Press, 1958)

Social Policy & Administration by D. V. Donnison & Others (George Allen & Unwin, Ltd., 1965)

The Professional Houseparent by Eva Burmeister (Columbia Univ. Press, 1960)

Children in Need by Anthony Denney (SCM Press, Ltd., 1966)

PAPERS, REPORTS ETC.

Whose Children? by Lady Allen of Hurtwood (The Favil Press, Ltd., 1944)

Report of the Committee on Homeless Children (*The 'Clyde' Report*) (H.M. Stationery Office, Edinburgh, 1946)

Report of the Care of Children Committee (The 'Curtis' Report)
(H.M. Stationery Office, London, 1946)
Children in Britain (H.M. Stationery Office, London, 1967)
Social Work (Scotland) Act 1968 (II.M. Stationery Office, London,
1968)

MANUSCRIPTS

Diaries of Admission, Discharge, etc. (Quarrier's Homes Archives,
1876/1970)
Minute Book of the Trustees of The Colony of Mercy etc. (Quarrier's
Homes Archives, 1903)
The William Quarrier School Log Books (Quarrier's Homes Archives,
1903)

ANNUAL REPORTS OF WILLIAM QUARRIER AND HIS SUCCESSORS

A Narrative of Facts Relative to Work Done for Christ (Quarrier's
Homes Archives, 1871/1970)